THE CONTINUING THREAT OF BOKO HARAM

JOINT HEARING

BEFORE THE

SUBCOMMITTEE ON AFRICA, GLOBAL HEALTH, GLOBAL HUMAN RIGHTS, AND INTERNATIONAL ORGANIZATIONS

AND THE

SUBCOMMITTEE ON TERRORISM, NONPROLIFERATION, AND TRADE

OF THE

COMMITTEE ON FOREIGN AFFAIRS HOUSE OF REPRESENTATIVES

ONE HUNDRED THIRTEENTH CONGRESS

FIRST SESSION

———

NOVEMBER 13, 2013

———

Serial No. 113–114

———

Printed for the use of the Committee on Foreign Affairs

Available via the World Wide Web: http://www.foreignaffairs.house.gov/ or http://www.gpo.gov/fdsys/

———

U.S. GOVERNMENT PRINTING OFFICE

85–552PDF   WASHINGTON : 2014

———

For sale by the Superintendent of Documents, U.S. Government Printing Office
Internet: bookstore.gpo.gov   Phone: toll free (866) 512–1800; DC area (202) 512–1800
Fax: (202) 512–2104   Mail: Stop IDCC, Washington, DC 20402–0001

COMMITTEE ON FOREIGN AFFAIRS

EDWARD R. ROYCE, California, *Chairman*

CHRISTOPHER H. SMITH, New Jersey
ILEANA ROS-LEHTINEN, Florida
DANA ROHRABACHER, California
STEVE CHABOT, Ohio
JOE WILSON, South Carolina
MICHAEL T. McCAUL, Texas
TED POE, Texas
MATT SALMON, Arizona
TOM MARINO, Pennsylvania
JEFF DUNCAN, South Carolina
ADAM KINZINGER, Illinois
MO BROOKS, Alabama
TOM COTTON, Arkansas
PAUL COOK, California
GEORGE HOLDING, North Carolina
RANDY K. WEBER SR., Texas
SCOTT PERRY, Pennsylvania
STEVE STOCKMAN, Texas
RON DeSANTIS, Florida
TREY RADEL, Florida
DOUG COLLINS, Georgia
MARK MEADOWS, North Carolina
TED S. YOHO, Florida
LUKE MESSER, Indiana

ELIOT L. ENGEL, New York
ENI F.H. FALEOMAVAEGA, American
  Samoa
BRAD SHERMAN, California
GREGORY W. MEEKS, New York
ALBIO SIRES, New Jersey
GERALD E. CONNOLLY, Virginia
THEODORE E. DEUTCH, Florida
BRIAN HIGGINS, New York
KAREN BASS, California
WILLIAM KEATING, Massachusetts
DAVID CICILLINE, Rhode Island
ALAN GRAYSON, Florida
JUAN VARGAS, California
BRADLEY S. SCHNEIDER, Illinois
JOSEPH P. KENNEDY III, Massachusetts
AMI BERA, California
ALAN S. LOWENTHAL, California
GRACE MENG, New York
LOIS FRANKEL, Florida
TULSI GABBARD, Hawaii
JOAQUIN CASTRO, Texas

AMY PORTER, *Chief of Staff*   THOMAS SHEEHY, *Staff Director*
JASON STEINBAUM, *Democratic Staff Director*

CONTENTS

THE CONTINUING THREAT OF BOKO HARAM

WEDNESDAY, NOVEMBER 13, 2013

House of Representatives,
Subcommittee on Africa, Global Health,
Global Human Rights, and International Organizations and
Subcommittee on Terrorism, Nonproliferation, and Trade,
Committee on Foreign Affairs,
Washington, DC.

The subcommittees met, pursuant to notice, at 1 o'clock p.m., in room 2200 Rayburn House Office Building, Hon. Christopher H. Smith (chairman of the Subcommittee on Africa, Global Health, Global Human Rights, and International Organizations) presiding.

Mr. SMITH. The hearing will come to order and good afternoon to everybody. Today's is a joint hearing of our subcommittees and I thank Chairman Poe for working so well with our subcommittee. This is of combined interest to the terrorism and of course, the Africa subcommittee.

Let me begin with my opening comments and then we will go to my distinguished colleagues and then, of course, to you, Madam Assistant Secretary.

Nigeria is one of the United States' main Africa trading partners and good friend, ally, and a major economic and political force beyond, even the African continent. Unfortunately, it continues to be plagued by terrorist forces whose reach extends beyond the borders of that country. Today's hearing is intended to examine the extent to which the organization known as Boko Haram and its affiliates pose a threat to Nigeria, and the region, as well as the United States and the rest of the international community.

Boko Haram is a Nigerian terrorist organization whose full name in Arabic means "People Committed to the Propagation of the Prophet's Teachings and Jihad." The name Boko Haram is a translation meaning that conventional education, Boko, is forbidden. Because of its repeated attacks against Christian targets, especially holy days such as Christmas and Easter. Boko Haram is seen by some as principally anti-Christian. In the last year alone, Boko Haram terrorists are believed to have killed some 1,200 Christians in Nigeria. In fact, it is estimated that 60 percent of Christians killed worldwide because of religious intolerance die in Nigeria.

According to Mr. Emmanuel Obege, one of our witnesses who will be testifying shortly, 53 Christian churches have been attacked and 216 people have been murdered by terrorists in those churches. However, it would not be a completely accurate interpretation of the facts to assume that what is happening in Nigeria is just a

Muslim-Christian conflict. In the past 2 years, both of our sub-committees have sent staff delegations to investigate the Boko Haram threat.

And this past September, Gregory Simpkins, our subcommittee staff director, and I visited Abuja and Jos to further look into this matter. We found that the truth of this organization is much more complex than is widely understood. Although exact numbers were not made available to us, Boko Haram is definitely targeting other Muslims who don't agree with their views. Muslim pastors who criticized the terrorists' violence are themselves made targets. We were told by some that if an imam or some teacher in a mosque speaks out against Boko Haram on a Friday, he will be targeted for death on Saturday. What must be prevented in a growing inability for Christians and Muslims to work together to meet their common threat. And we found enormous examples, numerous examples I should say, of cooperation between Christian and Muslim leaders to combat this killing spree by Boko Haram.

According to various reports, Boko Haram began in 2003, when about 200 university students and unemployed youth created a camp in Yobe State near the Niger border to withdraw from what they considered the corrupt, simple, and unjust Nigerian Government and their community was supposedly founded on Islamic law. The group was also known by the nickname the "Nigerian Taliban." Violent clashes with Nigerian security forces destroyed the group several times, but its charismatic leader, Mohammed Yusuf, kept the group alive until his death while in police custody in July 2009. Since Yusuf's death, there have been various spokes-men, but one person who is believed to be the nominal leader, Abubakar Shekau. Further, a breakaway group known as Ansaru, has appeared on the scene.

The proliferation of voices speaking for Boko Haram and the new faction leads some to believe that this is not a coherent organization. We learned that it is actually a very sophisticated organization, operating in cells disconnected from each other, but coordinating at a high level. While there are some acting in the name of Boko Haram for their own purposes, this terrorist group is organized, albeit in an unconventional manner.

Some also believe that this group is purely a domestic terrorist group operating in Nigeria. We found that to be a false assumption as well. Boko Haram and Ansaru do wage attacks on the Nigerian Government and other domestic targets. Nevertheless, their actions prove their participation in the global jihad movement that wages violent war worldwide to establish their skewed version of Islam as the prevailing religion globally. Various actions such as the bomb-ing of the United Nations office in Abuja in August 2011, and nu-merous statements from Boko Haram's spokesmen indicate their international intent. This international focus has been confirmed by both American and Nigerian intelligence information.

The three criteria for an organization to be declared a foreign terrorist organization by the U.S. Government are (1) it must be a foreign organization; (2) engage in terrorist activity; (3) it must threaten the security of the United States nationals, U.S. national security, or the economic interests of the United States. Clearly,

Boko Haram/Ansaru meets that test and we do welcome the news that was announced earlier today.

I have introduced HR 3209 which urged the administration to declare Boko Haram a foreign terrorist organization. This measure would provide tools for stopping those who currently provide funding for others in their murderous, terrorist organizations that they run. And again, we welcome the State Department's statement today that they will declare Boko Haram an FTO.

Our Government has provided training and other assistance to the Nigerian Government to battle this terrorist threat. Unfortunately, the past brutally demonstrated by the Nigerian security forces, as well as the inability of Nigerian security forces to collaborate with one another, have prevented their effort from being as successful as it should be. In far too many cases, the Nigerian Government itself has actually turned local people in the North against its effort to win the terrorist threat. By that ineffectiveness, the Nigerian security forces have pushed Nigerian Christians and Muslims to form their own militias to protect themselves from terrorists and each other. In the long run, this development makes eventual reconciliation of Nigeria's various religious and ethnic communities even more difficult.

We have with us today the administration's point person for our Government's effort to help end the terrorist threats to Nigeria; a leading Nigerian spokesman against this terrorism; a Nigerian Christian expert on this terrorist threat; and an American-based expert on this violence; and a survivor of the Boko Haram threat that Greg and I met when we were in Jos. This survivor, Mr. Adamu, was challenged to renounce his Christian faith. When he refused, he was shot right through the mouth, right through the lower part of his face and left for dead, bleeding. Miraculously, he survived and joins us today, one of the most inspiring examples of faith because he was told "renounce your faith and you will live, if you don't, you will die." And so a man that has unbelievable courage as well as faith. He says, "I have a message to everyone that will hear my story. Do everything that you can to end this ruthless religious persecution in northern Nigeria."

I now would like to yield to Ms. Bass for any opening comments she may have.

Ms. BASS. Thank you, Mr. Chairman, Chairman Poe and Ranking Member Sherman. I want to thank you for your leadership in calling today's hearing and I want to extend my greetings and welcome to the Assistant Secretary. I believe this is your first time you are coming to testify in your current capacity, but we will give you a more proper welcome next week, so welcome.

Nigeria is a critical, strategic partner for the United States. As Africa's most populous nation and with an economy that has the potential to be the largest on the continent, it is important politically, economically, and socially. Its importance cannot be overstated.

We know that this is the reason for the hearing today in focusing on Boko Haram. There is no question that Boko Haram presents an important and critical security challenge for Nigeria, West Africa, and I believe the continent as a whole. The frequency of attacks, its reach and the brutality and the lethal dimension of those attacks are a serious problem that must be addressed.

Since 2010, the scale of attacks by Boko Haram have led to the deaths of nearly 4,000 people including children. The group has used car bombs, improvised explosive devices, and suicide attacks to exact a heavy and unforgiving toll on the Nigerian people. Boko Haram has attacked churches, schools, police stations, and places where civilians are known to frequent including bars and markets.

While Boko Haram's attacks can in no way be justified, we do know that their long-standing grievances that may be leading to young men being recruited into their ranks. The slow pace of development in Nigeria's north including that of infrastructure development, jobs, and greater investments in the region, have if not a direct result, may be at least partially to blame. We have seen similar frustrations across the continent, particularly in Somalia where large numbers of young people, desperate for opportunities have found negative outlets like al-Shabaab.

As the Nigerian Government has rightly moved to address the internal threat of Boko Haram, the international community has been critical over concerns over human rights abuses. While civilians have not been the target of efforts to fight Boko Haram, civilians have nonetheless been caught in the violent middle ground.

I want to conclude by saying that I am keenly aware of the various sides that seek a greater and more executing response by our Government. As the Assistant Secretary will share, I know we continue to consult with Nigerian authorities on a range of efforts to ensure that Boko Haram, its leaders and fighters are held accountable for past, and any future attempts to destabilize the Nigerian Government and its brazen attacks on civilians. And in this, we look forward for all and new opportunities to stop Boko Haram from further expansion and further violence.

Thank you, and I look forward to the hearing.

Mr. SMITH. Thank you, Ms. Bass. I would like to now yield to the co-chairman of this hearing, the chairman of the Subcommittee on Terrorism, Nonproliferation, and Trade, the distinguished gentleman from Texas, Mr. Poe.

Mr. POE. I thank the gentleman for yielding. Boko Haram is a vicious terrorist group that carries out daily attacks against the Nigerian people. They target Christians, moderate Muslims as well. They kill in the name of religion. They promote anarchy.

This past summer, I sent my staff to Nigeria in early August to get a sense of the situation on the ground. What they found was alarming, sobering, and inhumane. Boko Haram finds it roots in the keenly conservative north of Nigeria. After its leader was killed in 2009, Boko went underground, but they emerged in 2010 as a more radical and violent group led by a vicious killer named Shekau. They attacked Christians on Christmas Day 2010, Christmas Day 2011, Christmas in 2012. Eighty-six people were killed on 2010; 42 in 2011; and 12 on 2012.

Mass beheadings, child soldiers, and forced marriages of local women to Boko Haram members are now more commonplace. Boko Haram's mystique is furthered by social media users who spread their propaganda statements among jihadists wannabes and people who just want to kill other people. The group was responsible for a 2010 prison break that freed 700 prisoners and a bombing of the city of Jos that killed more than 80 people. In 2011, Boko bombed a police headquarters in the Nigerian capital of Abuja and carried out a massive suicide attack against the U.N. headquarters there.

This year, just a few weeks ago on September 29th, it targeted an agricultural college and killed 40 students in a dormitory. Some say that the Nigerian military's heavy-handed response simply adds fuel to the fire of Boko Haram's recruitment. Everyone agrees that corruption does hamper the military's efforts. It means that the general population is frustrated that they do not receive basic services like education and healthcare. It also means that the economy in many parts of the country is not doing well because there are not enough basic infrastructure like roads and schools. And that makes recruitment for Boko Haram even easier.

When it comes to fighting the Boko Haram, the military is corrupt and there is no money left over to pay the salaries of the soldiers that actually do the fighting. In addition to Boko Haram, Nigeria also has a more extremist offshoot terrorist group called Ansaru. This group is closely allied to al-Qaeda and may seek to strike targets outside of Nigeria's borders. Boko Haram has embraced international jihad with its attacks on the U.N. and Abuja. In 2011, the former commander of the U.S. Africa Command said that Boko Haram was in contact with AQIM and al-Shabaab. We ought to be on the lookout for increasing international agenda for this terrorist organization. Boko fighters go to Mali and Cameroon to train and get weapons and munitions. As a result of pressure from the military, reports show that the terrorist group may be spreading in small numbers to economic centers in the south. Boko Haram sustains itself, finances its killings by kidnapping for ransom, extortion, taxation, protection rackets, smuggling, and any type of criminal enterprise that they can think of. Boko Haram isn't rolling in dough, but it doesn't take that much money to wage an insurgency. This is one of the reasons why I support the State Department's designation today of Boko Haram as a foreign terrorist organization. It is long overdue. We need to apply all the tools that we have to stop these terrorists. Now that Boko Haram has been designated, we need to uncover their financial operations and force this designation and go after these outlaws.

We look forward to the hearing from our witnesses on the threat from Boko Haram. I yield back.

Mr. SMITH. Thank you, Chairman Poe. Ranking Member Sherman.

Mr. SHERMAN. Thank you for holding this hearing. I have been told Boko Haram means ''Western education is sinful'' in the Hausa language. That may differ a little bit from the linguist derivation provided by the gentleman from New Jersey, so our witness will tell us the linguistic derivation. But in any case, it is an Islamist group based in northeast Nigeria that seeks to establish Sharia law.

Over the past decade, Boko Haram has killed thousands, attacking Christians, bombing churches, attacking schools, police stations, and attacking other Muslims as well.

The State Department has offered a $7 million reward for the capture of one of Boko Haram's top leaders. This is a reprehensible organization that has attacked Christians during Christmas, at Easter; attacked Muslims who do not join in their bloody philosophy.

Now conflicts between Christians and Muslims of Nigeria are not new and preceded the creation of Boko Haram. Even the 1960s Civil War involving the attempt to create an independent Biafra stem in part from the way Christians were treated, particularly, Ibo traders were treated in northern Nigeria.

In more recent decades, Islamic groups have grown, especially in the north. Since the death of Mohammed Yusuf in 2009, the charismatic leader of Boko Haram, the group has split. Another group, Ansaru, announced its existence in 2012. The two groups are described as loosely coordinating under a joint council. I want to commend the State Department for classifying both Boko Haram and Ansaru as terrorist organizations. That is to say adding them to the list of the foreign terrorist organizations under—and also as especially designated global terrorists.

In September 2011, then commander of AFRICOM, General Ham stated that three African terrorist organizations, Shabaab in Somalia, al-Qaeda, Islamic Maghreb across the Sahel, and Boko Haram have explicitly and publicly voiced an intent to target Westerners and especially the United States.

Now I am going to drift a little bit from the exact subject here because our entire national security establishment has picked up a new phrase, pivot toward Asia, which sounds like it is going to mean more trade delegations to Tokyo and more Chinese language courses in our universities. But what I fear it really means is deciding that the fight with Islamist extremists in Africa and the Middle East is either over or is inconvenient. And redirecting all of our national security efforts toward confronting China in the South China Sea. Already, the Pentagon is shifting is research proposals. They are only interested in research that will help them shoot down Chinese planes or sink Chinese aircraft carriers.

Islamic extremism and the problems in North Africa and West Asia and all of Africa and the Middle East cannot be ignored just because there is a dispute over some islands off the coast of China. And pivoting toward Asia sounds to be like trying to find a higher technology, more conventional foe for a national security establishment that is frustrated by the difficulties of dealing with opponents that do not wear uniforms. It is time for us to pivot toward Africa, the Middle East and West and South Asia where Islamic extremism still poses a threat to the United States, notwithstanding bin Laden, and I yield back.

Mr. SMITH. Thank you, Mr. Chairman. I would like to now welcome our distinguished Ambassador Linda Thomas-Greenfield, just briefly, Ambassador Thomas-Greenfield is a member of the career Foreign Service and was sworn in on August 6, 2013 as Assistant Secretary for African Affairs. Prior to assuming her current position, as Director General she ran or led a team of about 400 employees who carried out personnel functions for the State Department's 60,000 strong work force. Since beginning her Foreign Service career in 1982, she has risen through the ranks to the minister consular level. Overseas, she has served in Jamaica, Nigeria, The Gambia, Kenya, Pakistan and at the U.S. Mission to the U.N. And as a matter of fact, we were just reminiscing, of course, I met the Ambassador there when we were working on refugee issues and she walked point on those issues so much so that in 2000, she got the Warren Christopher Award for Outstanding Achievement in Global Affairs in recognition of her work on behalf of refugees. She also served as Ambassador to Liberia where she served from 2008 to 2012.

Madam Ambassador, the floor is yours.

STATEMENT OF THE HONORABLE LINDA THOMAS–GREEN-FIELD, ASSISTANT SECRETARY, BUREAU OF AFRICAN AF-FAIRS, U.S. DEPARTMENT OF STATE

Ambassador THOMAS-GREENFIELD. Thank you very much. Chairman Smith, Chairman Poe, Ranking Member Bass, Ranking Member Sherman, other members of the committee, let me thank you for this opportunity to update you about our policy in Nigeria and specifically on our efforts to help Nigeria counter the threat of Boko Haram and other associated violent extremist groups.

I will provide a full copy of my written testimony so this will be somewhat abbreviated so that I leave enough time to take questions.

Chairman Smith and Chairman Poe, instability in Nigeria is of direct concern to the United States. Nigeria is one of our most important partners in Africa. It is home to an estimated 170 million people, making it the most populous country in Africa and the seventh most populous country in the world. Nigeria has the 22nd fastest-growing economy in the world, the 13th largest supply of oil to the global market, and the second largest destination for U.S. private investment in Africa. Nigeria is also the second largest Africa contributor to U.N. peacekeeping operations around the world, not just in Africa, but around the world, and we welcome Nigeria's participation on the U.N. Security Council beginning in January.

The significant mutual interests we share with Nigeria have led us to build a robust, bilateral relationship which we have deepened and broadened through the U.S.-Nigeria Binational Commission. We meet regularly with senior Nigerian officials. President Obama met with President Jonathan in New York in September on the margins of the U.N. General Assembly. Under Secretary Sherman led a large interagency U.S. delegation to Abuja in mid-August to discuss civilian security with senior Nigerian civilian and military leaders, including President Jonathan and National Security Advisor Dasuki. I will be traveling myself to Nigeria in December and hope to have meetings at those same levels.

Additionally, I would like to thank you, Congressman Smith for your visit to Nigeria in September to meet with Nigerians affected by Boko Haram's violence. It is through these engagements, ours and yours, that we are able to translate our partnership into mutual action to advance opportunities and address threats that Boko Haram poses.

Boko Haram and associated violent extremist groups, such as the faction known as Ansaru, that you all described in so much detail to us, pose a threat to Nigeria's stability. These groups attack the Nigerian Government. They attack the military. They attack ordinary citizens of all walks of life, including numerous Christians, but even a greater number of Muslims. Their actions have increased tensions between ethnic communities. It has interrupted development, frightened investors, and alarmed Nigeria's neighbors. Boko Haram and associated groups can strike Nigeria's neighbors and it targets foreigners. Their unspeakable violence has killed too many Nigerians to even count, as we saw during September, when attackers in Benisheikh shot more than 160 people and in Yobe, where you described earlier, more than fifty innocent students lost their lives.

In August 2011, a suicide bomber from Boko Haram attacked the United Nations headquarters in Nigeria's capital Abuja. And on February 19 of this year, Boko Haram kidnapped seven French tourists in Cameroon. And although Boko Haram has directed most of its violence and rhetoric at Nigerian targets reports of linkages between Boko Haram and al-Qaeda in the Islamic Maghreb, or AQIM, are very worrisome for us as well as for the Nigerians.

Boko Haram's violence comes at a time of uncertainty and tension for Nigeria. Preparations for the country's 2015 elections have already begun, and political realignments are adding to existing tensions. In the oil-producing Niger Delta region, thieves steal at least 100,000 barrels of oil per day and perhaps much more. This theft reduces government revenues, fuels corruption and international crime, and contributes to environmental degradation. Corruption hinders the country's efforts to enforce the rule of law, to attract investment, and expand infrastructure. Good governance, healthy political competition, equitable economic growth would go a long way to address all of these challenges. And the strategy of countering Boko Haram should be, in other words, holistic. The government needs not only to stop Boko Haram's attacks, but address longstanding grievances of law-abiding northern Nigerians about government corruption and unfairness that attracts disaffected youth to Boko Haram.

Military and law enforcement efforts are necessary, but they alone are insufficient to counter the threat posed by Boko Haram and associated violent extremist groups. In the long run, reducing Boko Haram's ability to recruit is just as important as degrading its capabilities. Nigeria must protect civilians. It must guarantee human rights, and ensure accountability in instances where government officials and security forces violate those rights. Nigeria must demonstrate to all Nigerians that government can be and must be the sole, trusted arbiter of justice in the country.

The United States is committed to helping the Nigerian Government and people counter the threat of Boko Haram. In June 2012, the State Department designated Boko Haram's top commander as specially designated global terrorist under Section 1(b) of Executive Order 13224. In June 2013, the State Department added Abubakar Shekau, Boko Haram's official leader, to our Rewards for Justice Program. I am pleased also to announce that the United States has taken additional steps to counter the threat posed by Boko Haram and Ansaru. Earlier today, the State Department designated both as foreign terrorist organizations under Section 219 of the Immigration and Nationality Act, as amended, and especially Designated Global Terrorists under Section 1(b) of Executive Order 13224. We took this step after very careful consideration and I know you think it was too long, but we did make sure that we got it right. We anticipate that this designation will empower U.S. law enforcement and the Treasury Department with additional tools to pursue these violent extremist organizations. We believe this designation is an important and appropriate step, but again, it is only one tool in what we believe must be a comprehensive approach toward addressing the Boko Haram threat.

We are committed to assisting Nigeria in bolstering its law enforcement capabilities and ultimately in shifting to what we believe should be an integrated, civilian security-focused strategy to counter Boko Haram and Ansaru in a manner that adheres to the rule of law and ensures accountability and diminishes the ability of Boko Haram's appeal and legitimacy to civilian populations.

The United States recognizes that the Nigerian Government and security forces face a difficult challenge in countering the Boko Haram insurgency. Both ordinary citizens and security forces have suffered. Still, we are concerned by reports that some Nigerian security forces have committed gross human rights violations in response to Boko Haram. Not only because their approach is wrong, but because it is counterproductive. We have raised this concern with the Government of Nigeria at the highest levels. And while northern Nigerians, Muslims and Christians alike, largely reject Boko Haram's vision and violence, Boko Haram has exploited local resentment of these violations and other long-standing grievances against the central government to attract recruits.

Nigeria's prosperity and stability matter to all of Africa. The United States is committed to several Presidential initiatives in partnership with Nigeria, including the Young African Leaders Initiative and Power Africa, as well as significant programs in the areas of health, education, and economic growth. Nigeria's success is important to us. We must continue to help our Nigerian partners develop an effective, multi-faceted strategy toward Boko Haram. Overcoming the challenges posed by Boko Haram will not be easy and we know that, but we do believe it is possible. We appreciate all of your efforts here in Congress. We appreciate your interest in this issue and we are ready to work with you, as well as with the government and people of Nigeria in the months ahead to work against this threat. I look forward to your questions. Thank you very much.

[The prepared statement of Ambassador Thomas-Greenfield follows:]

Testimony of Ambassador Linda Thomas-Greenfield,

Assistant Secretary of State for African Affairs

before the

House Foreign Affairs Committee

Subcommittee on Africa, Global Health, Human Rights, and
International Organizations

and

Subcommittee on Terrorism, Nonproliferation, and Trade

"Countering the Threat Posed by Boko Haram"

November 13, 2013

Chairman Smith, Chairman Poe, Ranking Member Bass, Ranking

Member Deutch, and Members of the Committee, thank you for this

opportunity to update you about U.S. policy on Nigeria and specifically

our efforts to help Nigeria counter the threat posed by Boko Haram and

associated violent extremist groups.

Chairman Smith and Chairman Poe, instability in Nigeria is of

direct concern to the United States. Nigeria is one of our most important

partners in Africa. It is home to an estimated 170 million people,

making it the most populous country in Africa and the seventh most

populous country in the world. Nigeria is the twenty-second fastest-growing economy in the world, the thirteenth-largest supplier of oil to the global market, and the second largest destination for U.S. private investment in Africa. Nigeria is also the second-largest African contributor to UN peacekeeping operations around the world and we welcome Nigeria's participation on the U.N. Security Council beginning in January.

The significant mutual interests we share with Nigeria have led us to build a robust bilateral relationship, which we have deepened and broadened through the U.S.-Nigeria Binational Commission. We meet regularly with senior Nigerian officials. President Obama met with President Jonathan on the margins of the UN General Assembly in September. Under Secretary Wendy Sherman led a large interagency U.S. delegation to Abuja in mid-August to discuss civilian security with senior Nigerian civilian and military leaders, including President Jonathan and National Security Advisor Dasuki. Additionally, we have welcomed the travel of Congressional partners like Chairman Smith who visited Nigeria September 21-24 to meet with Nigerians affected by Boko Haram violence. It is through these engagements that we are able to translate our partnership into mutual action to advance opportunities and address threats.

Boko Haram and associated violent extremist groups, such as the faction known as Ansaru, pose a threat to Nigeria's stability. These groups attack the Nigerian government, military, and ordinary citizens of all walks of life, including numerous Christians and an even greater number of Muslims. Their actions have increased tensions between ethnic communities, interrupted development, frightened investors, and alarmed Nigeria's neighbors. Boko Haram and associated groups can strike Nigeria's neighbors and target foreigners. Their unspeakable violence has killed too many Nigerians, as we saw during September, when attacks in Benisheikh shot more than 160 people and in Yobe, where more than fifty innocent students lost their lives. In August 2011, a suicide bomber from Boko Haram attacked the United Nations headquarters in Nigeria's capital Abuja. On February 19 of this year, Boko Haram kidnapped seven French tourists in Cameroon. Although Boko Haram has directed most of its violence and rhetoric at Nigerian targets, reports of linkages between Boko Haram and Al Qa'ida in the Islamic Maghreb, or AQIM, are worrying.

The ongoing violence in northern Nigeria has multiple causes. These include Boko Haram's ideology, which opposes Western culture and education and seeks to overthrow the Nigerian state and replace it with a regime enforcing strict shari'a law. Boko Haram has exploited religious rhetoric in an attempt to justify its violence, casting the state as hopelessly corrupt and un-Islamic. Regional and socioeconomic disparities have also contributed to the group's ability to recruit. Northern Nigeria has long lagged behind the south in education and economic development. In 2011, Nigeria's national unemployment rate was 24 percent, but the unemployment rate in six of the twelve far northern states exceeded 30 percent. In 2010, Nigeria's rate of absolute poverty was 62 percent, but in eight of the twelve far northern states the figure exceeded 70 percent. Of Nigeria's estimated 10.5 million children who do not attend school, 92 percent are estimated to be in the north. Boko Haram's activities call our attention not just to violence, but also to poverty and inequality in Nigeria.

Boko Haram's violence also comes at a time of uncertainty and tension for Nigeria. Preparations for the country's 2015 elections have already begun, and political realignments are adding to existing tensions. In the oil-producing Niger Delta region, thieves steal at least 100,000 barrels of oil per day and perhaps much more. This theft reduces government revenues, fuels corruption and international crime, and contributes to environmental degradation. In Nigeria's ethnically and religiously diverse Middle Belt, communal violence occurs in tragic cycles, overwhelming civilian authorities and stoking regional tensions. Corruption hinders the country's efforts to enforce the rule of law, generate electricity, attract investment, and expand infrastructure. Despite its tremendous wealth and vast human resources, Nigeria struggles to reduce poverty; despite its oil exports and agricultural riches, the country imports gasoline and rice. Good governance, healthy political competition, and equitable economic growth would go a long way to address all of these challenges. The strategy for countering Boko Haram should be, in other words, holistic. The government needs to not only stop Boko Haram's attacks, but address longstanding grievances of law-abiding northern Nigerians about government corruption and unfairness that attracts disaffected youth to Boko Haram.

The United States is committed to helping the Nigerian government and people counter the threat posed by Boko Haram and associated violent extremist groups. In recent years, we have worked to help isolate Boko Haram's leaders. In June 2012, the State Department designated Boko Haram's top commanders as Specially Designated Global Terrorists under section 1(b) of Executive Order 13224. In June 2013, the State Department added Abubakar Shekau, Boko Haram's official leader, to our Rewards for Justice Program and offered up to $7 million for information leading to his location.

I am pleased to inform you that the United States has recently taken additional steps to counter the threat posed by Boko Haram and Ansaru. Earlier today, the State Department designated both as Foreign Terrorist Organizations under Section 219 of the Immigration and Nationality Act, as amended, and as Specially Designated Global Terrorists under section 1(b) of Executive Order 13224. We took this step after careful consideration. We anticipate that this designation will empower U.S. law enforcement and the Treasury Department with additional tools to pursue these violent extremist organizations. We believe this designation is an important and appropriate step, but it is only one tool in what we believe must be a comprehensive approach toward addressing the Boko Haram threat. It is also our sincere hope that the Nigerian government and people will see this as a gesture of support in their fight against Boko Haram. We are committed to assisting Nigeria in bolstering its law enforcement capabilities and ultimately shifting to an integrated civilian-security-focused strategy to counter Boko Haram and Ansaru in a manner that adheres to the rule of law and ensures accountability.

The United States has also sought to enhance the capacity of Nigeria and its neighbors to detect, disrupt, respond to, investigate, and prosecute terrorist incidents. Through the Trans-Sahara Counterterrorism Partnership, we build military, law enforcement, and civilian capacity and resilience across the Sahel and Maghreb regions to counter terrorism. We continue to train and equip Nigerian law enforcement units to strengthen leadership, improve crisis management, enhance investigations and forensics, and counter improvised explosive devices. The State Department also funds a Legal Adviser to help the Nigerian government strengthen its anti-money laundering and counter terrorist financing regime.

Military and law enforcement efforts are necessary, but they alone are insufficient to counter the threat posed by Boko Haram and associated violent extremist groups. In the long run, reducing Boko Haram's ability to recruit is just as important as degrading its capabilities. In addition to the imperatives of improving governance and fostering equitable development, Nigeria must protect civilians, guarantee human rights, and ensure accountability in instances where government officials and security forces violate those rights. Nigeria must demonstrate that government can be the sole, trusted arbiter of justice in the country.

The United States recognizes that the Nigerian government and security forces face a difficult challenge in countering the Boko Haram insurgency. Both ordinary citizens and security forces have suffered. Still, we are concerned by reports that some Nigerian security forces have committed gross human rights violations in response to Boko Haram. We have raised this concern with the Government of Nigeria at the highest levels. While northern Nigerians, Muslims and Christians alike, largely reject Boko Haram's vision and violence, Boko Haram has exploited local resentment of these violations and other long-standing grievances against the central government to attract recruits.

The United States is committed to helping Nigeria shift to a strategy that focuses on protecting citizens. Such a strategy would diminish Boko Haram's appeal and legitimacy. We support civil society-led efforts in Nigeria that counter Boko Haram's narrative and its violent extremist message. We also seek to increase outreach with youth leaders in northern Nigeria, and to promote better relations between these leaders and Nigerian government officials. We maintain an American corner in Kano, Nigeria, although its outreach activities have been limited by the security situation.

Nigeria's prosperity and stability matter to all of Africa. The United States is committed to several Presidential initiatives in partnership with Nigeria, including the Young African Leaders Initiative and Power Africa, as well as significant programs for health and

economic growth. Nigeria's success is important to us. We must

continue to help our Nigerian partners develop an effective, multi-

faceted strategy toward Boko Haram. Overcoming the challenges posed

by Boko Haram will not be easy, but we believe it is possible with

leadership and creativity. We appreciate Congress' interest in this issue,

and we are ready to work with you in the months ahead. I look forward

to your questions.

———————

Mr. SMITH. Thank you very much, Madam Ambassador.

Mr. SHERMAN. There is a vote on the floor.

Mr. SMITH. I know. We do have a series of votes, but I thought we would start some of the questions and I do hope your time permits you because I know many members do have very significant questions so I thank you for that and for our other witnesses as well, for your patience.

Let me begin the questioning. First, thank you for the designation of FTO. I think that is monumental, it is historic, and it is absolutely warranted. I remember in July 2012 asking Ambassador Carson a number of questions and there was a great deal of resistance. As a matter of fact, he said that the bulk of the organization, we believe to be mainly aimed at going after Nigerians and that is not good either, of course, but they certainly have shown that they meet the criteria; this is absolutely well deserved and hopefully will make a difference.

You might want to for the committee and for all, maybe to delineate as to what that actually means. Meeting with Members of the Congress, House and Senate in Abuja, as well as here, when they visited, some thought it might be a mark, a bad mark against the country of Nigeria and I and others tried to say, no, this is only targeted at a group of terrorists and thugs who are murdering people inside as well as those who are visiting in Nigeria, that is to say, Boko Haram is doing that. So what is actually the positiveness of that designation?

Secondly, your view of Goodluck Jonathan's military efforts to contain, combat, and hopefully end this terrible scourge in Nigeria, Boko Haram. The Leahy amendment, as we all know, is all about vetting and human rights criteria, but if you could speak to whether or not you believe there needs to be a revisiting of at least its application, which can become counterproductive. Whole groups are being disqualified simply because of a concern that it might now comport with the Leahy amendment and it seems to me that needs to be looked at very carefully. Don't ever, obviously, enable a human rights abuser, but when it gets in the way of good, solid training forces who could be more efficacious on the battlefield, but also be very pro-human rights, it seems to me that that is both in Nigeria's as well as our best interest.

And finally, on the issue of the persecution of Christians, I met with a group of Christians in Jos who were refugees, IDPs, and they said that their homes were actually marked in kind of a perverse reversal of the Passover and it said ''infidel'' on the top of their doors and that night Boko Haram wielding AK–47s, individuals, came and killed people. Some got out, others did not. And again, as I mentioned, one of our witnesses, Mr. Adamu, when I heard his story, I was in tears. I am not moved to tears easily, but I welled up with tears as he talked about his faith as a Christian, as they blew his face away and left him for dead, right in front of his dear wife, who was sobbing, but rather than convert, he stood up. That kind of atrocity against Christians or anyone, obviously, is unconscionable. If you could speak to that as well, those two questions.

Ambassador THOMAS-GREENFIELD. Thank you. Let me start with your first question, what does the designation mean? I have to tell you that we got a very positive response when we informed the Nigerians that we had made the decision to designate. It sends a strong message to the people of Nigeria that we feel their pain and that we understand what is going on in Nigeria. And the message has been very, very positive from the Nigeria front.

The designation gives us some additional tools for providing support to the Nigerians particularly, through Treasury, putting holds on bank accounts and movements of cash, but also in terms of our ability to provide additional support to Nigeria and to countries in the regions to help them fight Boko Haram. Nigeria itself declared Boko Haram a terrorist organization earlier this year. The UK has done the same and now we have joined them and I am pleased that that has happened.

In terms of the government's effort, we know that the Nigerian Government has a tough job responding to this crisis. And as I said in my testimony, they have not always gotten it right. They have been particularly heavy handed in the response. I think with the hope and desire that they will bring this to an end quickly. It has not come to an end quickly and some of the Nigerian military forces in their heavy-handed use of force have committed some human rights violations that we have raised with the government and because of that, some of their troops have been under Leahy, not allowed to get training in the United States or provided by the United States.

So we are hopeful that through our continued work with the government we can help them address some of their approach so that the violations are not continued. We are encouraging them to allow international organizations and local NGOs to go into some of the detention centers to help them. And we are encouraging them not to do anything that would turn the people of the north against them. And we are hopeful that in the coming weeks in our visits and discussions with the government that we will be able to help them address some of these issues.

In terms of the persecution of Christians, the news on that front, we have all seen it. We all feel it. And we are all really disgusted by it. I would add that in addition the Boko Haram is a terrorist organization. And terrorist organizations harm everyone and they have killed, as they have killed Christians in the name of Islam, they have also killed Muslims in the name of Islam. And I make that point because their victims are across the board. It is women and children. It is government officials. It is civilians. It is Nigerians. It is across the border in Niger, in Cameroon. It is French citizens being kidnapped. So while they do have a religious bent to what they do, they are nondiscriminating in their attacks on people. And what that means is we have to work to stop this.

Mr. SMITH. But I think you would agree that there has been absolutely disproportionate focus on Christians. As a matter of fact, Mr. Emmanuel Ogebe, who is the managing partner of U.S.-Nigeria Law Group, has been critical of the State Department, and I would agree, for downplaying the religious nature of this. And I, too, believe and know that Muslims are targeted. No doubt about it. But it is usually when they speak out against Boko Haram. But Christians are targeted simply because of their faith. So you would agree with that?

Ambassador THOMAS-GREENFIELD. Yes, sir.

Mr. SMITH. Thank you. We will stand in brief recess. There are three votes, an interim, and then two more votes, but we will come back during that interim and it will be in about 15 to 20 minutes. Thank you for patience.

Ambassador THOMAS-GREENFIELD. Thank you.

[Off the record.]

Mr. SMITH. The subcommittees will resume their hearing and their seating. And again, I apologize to all of our witnesses and to you, Madam Ambassador, for that lengthy series of votes, but I now yield to the distinguished chairman, Mr. Poe.

Mr. POE. Thank you, Mr. Chairman. Thank you for being here. I am not always one who gives kudos to the State Department, but I think you are doing a great job representing the interests of the United States. That is my opinion.

I have a few questions, of course. The Nigerian military, I just need your opinion, do they have the capability right now to defeat Boko Haram?

Ambassador THOMAS-GREENFIELD. That is a tough question. I think the Nigerian military has the capability to defeat Boko Haram. I think that they could use some support. It is a challenging job and one that we are prepared to help them with in terms of providing them with additional training, particularly in providing them with—and not just the military, with other security forces, with providing them with forensic support, investigation support, and other types of support. We think that their approach, again, has been somewhat heavy handed, I think, in an effort to bring this to closure quickly. And we have tried to work with them to help them address that issue. But it is not just a security issue. It is also an issue that requires the Nigerian Government to deal with some of the social and economic issues that exist in the north that has attracted people to Boko Haram. So being able to provide infrastructure, schools, the availability of healthcare, dealing with issues of corruption, all of those things go hand in hand with addressing the security issues that they are trying to deal with.

Mr. POE. Are we looking at a situation where the country may end up being a failed state because of the activities of Boko Haram? It seems like to me they promote anarchy. They want anarchy. They want people to live in fear and then you have the corruption with the government. Is that what the world has foreseen in Nigeria?

Ambassador THOMAS-GREENFIELD. I tend to be more optimistic. Nigeria is a huge country. It is a complex country. It is a country with tremendous diversity. I don't think Boko Haram has the power to make Nigeria into a failed state. There are lots of other elements that could contribute to that. Boko Haram will make Nigeria, particularly in the north, difficult to govern. Boko Haram will present challenges to security. It presents challenges to individuals who want to invest. It presents challenges to private American citizens who want to visit because we do have a travel warning out because of the activities of Boko Haram. But I don't think Boko Haram has the power to make Nigeria into a failed state.

Mr. POE. I have two more questions. On a related topic, there are many terrorist organizations, several that have been designated as foreign terrorist organizations. Do you have any information that Hezbollah or the Iranian Revolutionary Guards Corps is active in Nigeria?

Ambassador THOMAS-GREENFIELD. I don't have any information on those two organizations. I can go back and look at what we have and get an answer back to you. We do believe that Boko Haram has links to al-Qaeda. We think they have links to al-Shabaab. And we certainly think that they use the ideology of these organizations to support their efforts in Nigeria. But I have not seen anything to indicate that they have connections to Hezbollah or to Iran.

WRITTEN RESPONSE RECEIVED FROM THE HONORABLE LINDA THOMAS-GREENFIELD TO QUESTION ASKED DURING THE HEARING BY THE HONORABLE TED POE

We believe that it is highly unlikely that Boko Haram has any ties to Shia extremist organizations in Nigeria. We remain concerned about Hezballah and Iran attempting to extend influence in Africa by seeking support among sympathetic populations in Nigeria and elsewhere. We will continue to monitor potential nefarious activity in Nigeria and are following closely the May 2013 arrests and subsequent prosecution of the alleged Hezballah members in Nigeria.

Mr. POE. My understanding is they get their money from kidnapping, holding people for ransom, take over a little town and tax the citizens of the town, have protection rackets. They are involved in smuggling and anything else illegal they can think of. Will the designation of being an FTO, how will that affect the influx of money which is what they do, all that outlawry is what I call it. I am from Texas, so we call them outlaws. How will that affect, if it does, the money flow going to Boko Haram?

Ambassador THOMAS-GREENFIELD. I think the designation does give us some tools to track money that is going to Boko Haram. I doubt that their money is being put in legal instruments, so they generally get most of their funding through illegal means, through kidnappings, through other criminal activities. They certainly have had an impact on trade and the movement of goods in the north and probably have gotten some advantages from that. Again, I think it is through those activities that they have been able to fund their operations.

Mr. POE. Last question. What is your understanding as to the numbers? How many people are we talking about that consider themselves aligned with Boko Haram being their soldiers, their killers, whatever you want to call them? How many would you guess or estimate?

Ambassador THOMAS-GREENFIELD. Thank you for that question. And it is a question that I asked as I was preparing for this hearing. We don't have a real fix on what the numbers are. We think that the core of Boko Haram is not large, somewhere in the hundreds to thousands. But not in the tens of thousands, in the mid thousands. We think there are people who are sympathetic to Boko Haram in some of the communities they operate in, but an actual fix on the exact numbers, we are just not sure of.

Mr. POE. Thank you, Mr. Chairman.

Mr. SMITH. Thank you very much, Chairman Poe. Just a few final questions if I could, then hopefully others will return. If you could speak to, one of the things I noticed when Mr. Simpkins and I were in Jos was that the number of IDPs, 91 families that were housed in what looked like an old apartment or motel building, very cramped, very threadbare for any of the essentials that even in a refugee camp somebody might expect. I was struck by what seemed to be a lack of any resources for them either by the government or by the international community including USAID.

And I am wondering in his testimony, Mr. Ogebe, Emmanuel Ogebe, points out and this is his quote:

"U.S. has lagged behind in humanitarian assistance and has not provided anything to the victims of Boko Haram terrorism or crisis. Even less is said to the Federal Government about providing victim assistance."

What is your understanding as to what we are doing for those victims? I met with them. The kids all crowded around. They were desperate. They looked healthy, but thin. I am certainly frightened and again that is where we met one of our witnesses who will be talking or testifying a little bit later, Mr. Adamu, who told that story about being shot and being left for dead. Are we assisting?

Ambassador THOMAS-GREENFIELD. I think, as you know, Congressman, the U.S. is the largest contributor for humanitarian assistance worldwide, not just in the case of Nigeria. So we are assisting through international organizations, through NGOs, through our contributions. Unfortunately, our own presence is hampered by the security situation. We are not getting our people up to the North in a significant way. And I have heard just that, that people in the north are not seeing us. We had hoped to open a consulate in Kano. We actually had support for moving forward on that. We had staff identified, but because of security, we were not able to put them there. We have a small American Corners there, but again, we are not getting our people out there in a significant way.

We have one political officer and a public affairs officer based in Abuja and we are hoping that they can get out more and hoping that we can get more actual face on the ground in those regions so that people know we are there. They know we care. And they see the assistance that is coming through. But a lot of our assistance does not have our flag on it because we are going through international organizations.

Mr. SMITH. If you could, one, take back, the Jubilee Campaign was actually helping the people and those 91 refugees. And again their resources are tight. Any help from any of the faith-based groups? We actually met with a remarkable archbishop, Kaigama, who works side by side with the Muslim leadership in Jos. I mean it really was remarkable to see the kinds of things they are doing together to say that this is not Islam, and the Christians can work side by side with people of different faiths.

Ambassador THOMAS-GREENFIELD. I will definitely take that back.

Mr. SMITH. But he did tell us when we were meeting with him that he had a robust program to help AIDS orphans and it was canceled and could not get a good answer as to why, so I raised that when I went back to the Embassy. They didn't know and I still don't know. So if you could get that for us.

Ambassador THOMAS-GREENFIELD. We will follow up and get that answer.

WRITTEN RESPONSE RECEIVED FROM THE HONORABLE LINDA THOMAS-GREENFIELD TO QUESTION ASKED DURING THE HEARING BY THE HONORABLE CHRISTOPHER H. SMITH

The Centers for Disease Control (CDC) funded the Jos Catholic Archdiocese through a local partner organization, the AIDS Prevention Initiative in Nigeria (APIN). APIN's Community-Based Care and Support program finished on July 31, 2013. In October, another CDC partner—the Catholic organization Caritas—took over funding programs in the Archdiocese. So the program is once again being supported, although at a lower level than previously due to budget constraints.

Mr. SMITH. They had scores of AIDS orphans this faith-based organization was caring for that he has—they are going to somehow cobble together an assistance for them, basically. They don't have the money and they were getting it from us.

And I did ask a question and this is another take back, but I am a great believer, particularly in places like Nigeria where faith-based is so integral to the delivery of healthcare and other services. I asked how much of the PEPFAR money is being used or meted out to faith-based and I was told under 10 percent which I think is shocking. That needs to be turned around. And a day later, I am actually sitting with an archbishop outside of Abuja and he tells me how his program was cut and that was obviously a faith-based. And of course, they deal with all comers, Muslim, anyone who needs help as an orphan gets it. There is no test of faith for that kind of service. So I would ask if you could get back to us. That was very disconcerting.

Ambassador THOMAS-GREENFIELD. Thank you for bringing it to my attention. We will get back to you with an answer.

WRITTEN RESPONSE RECEIVED FROM THE HONORABLE LINDA THOMAS-GREENFIELD TO QUESTION ASKED DURING THE HEARING BY THE HONORABLE CHRISTOPHER H. SMITH

The U.S. Government PEPFAR team awards cooperative agreements, grants and contracts through full and open competition. Selection of current implementing partners was done through a competitive process. While 10% of the President's Emergency Program for AIDS Relief (PEPFAR)-funded activities in Nigeria are with faith-based organizations, the U.S. Government PEPFAR team in no way limits its engagement with faith-based organizations to a particular percentage or funding level.

Mr. SMITH. Let me just ask about child soldiers and Boko Haram and Ansaru. Do they coerce children to become soldiers and to what extent?

Ambassador THOMAS-GREENFIELD. We do have information to indicate that they are recruiting child soldiers. In terms of the fact that many young, particularly young men who are not in any formal education program go into some of the schools that are there that take them from their families and they are raised in these schools and they are used to go out in the streets to beg and they spend a lot of time getting inculcated with the ideas of Boko Haram. And we do know that they have used children in their efforts.

Mr. SMITH. The link of Boko Haram and Ansaru to other terrorist organizations, are you at liberty to——

Ambassador THOMAS-GREENFIELD. I am sorry. I didn't hear your question.

Mr. SMITH. Any links of Boko Haram and Ansaru to other terrorist organizations?

Ambassador THOMAS-GREENFIELD. As I said earlier, we do think that they do have links to AQIM. They certainly use their ideology, they use their operational plans and we know that they have done some training, particularly in Mali and in other areas, so the links are there. How close those links are, I can't discuss, but I think we are worried and concerned about those connections.

Mr. SMITH. Chairman Poe.

Mr. POE. I understand that the Leahy Law prevents us from training the Nigerian military in the north. Is that your understanding?

Ambassador THOMAS-GREENFIELD. All of those units that have been connected with human rights violations in the north have been, because of Leahy barred from any training by the U.S. Government, so that is correct.

Mr. POE. Does that include all of the military or just specific units of the Nigerian military?

Ambassador THOMAS-GREENFIELD. Those units that have been connected to human rights violations and I don't think at this point it is all the units, but I don't know that answer. I can get back to you on that.

WRITTEN RESPONSE RECEIVED FROM THE HONORABLE LINDA THOMAS-GREENFIELD TO QUESTION ASKED DURING THE HEARING BY THE HONORABLE TED POE

Assistance is withheld when the vetting process uncovers credible information that an individual or unit has committed a gross violation of human rights. We continue to provide assistance to other individuals and units of the Nigerian military.

Mr. POE. I would appreciate it if you get back to us and also more legalese about the Leahy Law and how it does apply or does not apply in this specific situation with the Nigeria military

Thank you, Mr. Chairman.

Mr. SMITH. I, too, would raise that as well. I understand the abundance of caution and that is prudent, but again, if we were in the position of training with human rights training, but also to be more effective, I think the Nigerian forces, some of the skills that might be imparted to them could make a huge difference.

I do want to thank Megan Ahearn who was our Foreign Service officer when Greg and I were in Nigeria. She was absolutely professional, effective, nonplused when our schedule changed by the minute and the Embassy was very supportive of the entire effort and the DCM Maria Brewer was also, even though she is relatively new there coming from a different posting, provided every courtesy and I am deeply appreciative of that as well.

Ambassador THOMAS-GREENFIELD. I will pass that on to her and I know it is a tough job because I have been your control officer before and you work really hard and we know that when you are coming, we have to be prepared for you. So to get that kind of kudos from you is really, really wonderful. So thank you.

Mr. SMITH. I know even the trip we made to Jos, they did not leave a single stone unturned in making it work in a safe way, but also a way that maximized every moment, so I want to thank her.

Ambassador THOMAS-GREENFIELD. Thank you.

Mr. SMITH. That would be Megan Ahearn.

Ambassador THOMAS-GREENFIELD. Thank you very much.

Mr. SMITH. Thank you, Madam Ambassador. I now would like to welcome to the witness table our second panel beginning with Mr. Emmanuel Obege who is an experienced attorney specializing in international matters, focusing on Nigeria. Exiled to the U.S. after becoming a political detainee during the brutal years of Nigeria's military dictatorship, Mr. Obege has played a role in shaping U.S. policy toward Nigeria and his quest for a more robust democracy. He has experience in managing, designing, and implementing complex international programs and projects in Nigeria. He presently is practicing as a legal consultant in Nigeria with the Washington, DC, bar and he holds the distinction of being the first specialist on Nigeria out of 100,000 lawyers licensed in Washington, DC.

Then Mr. Habila Adamu is from Yobe State in northern Nigeria and has experienced the brutality of Boko Haram himself. Unlike many others, he survived and fortunately he is able to be here to tell us about it today. Greg Simpkins and I met with him when we were traveling in Nigeria 2 months ago and I and all of us were deeply touched by his story. I believe his experience is emblematic of the experience of many Christians who are victimized by Boko Haram and his determination is a testament to his faith.

We will then hear from Mr. Jacob Zenn who is an expert on northern Nigerian security and a consultant on countering violent extremism. He is the author of the book, Northern Nigeria's Boko Haram, the Price in al-Qaeda's Africa Strategy, published in 2012 and based on his field work in Boko Haram's main area of operations in northern Nigeria, northern Cameroon, Chad, and southern Niger. He has briefed many officials with different governments and served as a policy advisor to the Nigerian-American Leadership Council which works with the Nigerian diaspora, U.S. Government, think tanks, and civic organizations to counter radicalization and to promote accountability.

Finally, we will hear from Dr. Guy Nzeribe who is an independent Africa-focused policy analyst with expertise in sectarian conflicts and terrorism in the southern Sahel zone and Nigeria. He is also an alumnus of the U.S. Defense Department's National Security Education Program at Georgetown University. Professionally, he has over 20 years of experience in politics, industry, and academia. He has worked in investment banking, consulting, technology, and is an international trade specialist. He is also a former college professor whose area of research and teaching focused on technology, management, and organizational change.

Mr. Ogebe.

STATEMENT OF MR. EMMANUEL OGEBE, MANAGING PARTNER, U.S.-NIGERIA LAW GROUP

Mr. OGEBE. Chairman Smith, I would like to thank you very much for hosting us today. I want to especially commend you for the courage in coming out to Nigeria. During your trip I learned that the security levels for Nigeria for U.S. dignitaries is equivalent to the levels for Iraq and for you to come out like that was really commendable.

Chairman Poe, I want to also thank you very much for co-hosting this session. I do want to say that in Nigeria, like in Texas, we still do outlaws. We call them outlaws and Boko Haram has been outlawed in Nigeria as well.

I want to say that I feel that Christmas came early for me today because the Secretary has done what was on my wish list a year ago. And she has taken the wind out of the sails of my presentation and so I will just make a few remarks.

The first thing is I would like to say for the last 3 years, we have been working aggressively to document what I call a ''pre-genocide'' in Nigeria. And this is what it looks like. Deborah Shatima had Boko Haram members come to her home. They shot her husband to death in front of her and when they were leaving, they abducted her seven and 9-year-old daughters and went away with them. Now this is horrific for any parent, but there is more. They came back 3 months later and said have you converted to Islam? She said no. And then they shot her remaining son and his friend and killed them.

Gentlemen, that is what terror looks like. Deborah Shatima has lived and known that terror for over a year now and while I am gratified that the State Department suddenly recognizes today that this is a foreign terrorist organization, we are concerned that it took them too long. However, we do want to give credit to this committee because we believe that the bill that you wrote finally nudged them to do the right thing.

Mr. Chairman, if I may, let me mention what the new face of Boko Haram terrorism looks like. While I was in Nigeria, shortly after you left, Boko Haram conducted a roadside massacre. And here is what they did. In Damaturu, only 5 out of 77 churches in that town remain open because Boko Haram has been attacking churches in such a massive manner. And many parts of Yobe State have been de-Christianized with Boko Haram exterminating vast neighborhoods by killing Christians from house to house, forcing massive population displacements.

This year, Boko Haram is now wiping out Christians in rural villages in Borno and burning the homes of those who have fled. Thousands are now refugees in Cameroon as we saw in our first-hand visit to the border of Cameroon. In fulfillment of a stated objective to eliminate Christians in northern Nigeria, Boko Haram has done significantly well since last year when it ordered Christians out. In Goza, Boko Haram has established camps in caves and mountains replicating the model of the Taliban of Afghanistan. Miles from our hotel, two churches were burned and the father of a gentleman we were interviewing was killed.

Deborah Shatima, as I mentioned, is still remaining, one of the few Christians remaining there. We have tried to move her out of there, but she still is remaining in the hope that her two girls who are now ten and eight might come home one day.

I want to say that with regard to the testimony of the Assistant Secretary who just spoke, there has been an improvement from the testimony last year. She has conceded that Boko Haram actually persecutes Christians, but she has again continued with this narrative that is not supported by the facts that more Muslims than Christians were killed. We are not interested in a game of numbers, but this is highly insensitive to the victims when the U.S. puts out gratuitous statements like that that are not reflective of what is going on on the ground. Considering that the United States has the largest political section in the African continent in Abuja, it is our hope that with the new personnel change there will be better reporting of the facts.

I want to mention again this so-called argument that it is economics that drives this brutality. The U.S. seems oblivious of the strong anti-American sentiment in much of the north where the U.S. liberation of Kuwait was riddled with riots as well as U.S. support for Israel amongst many other issues. After 9/11 bin Laden posters flooded northern Nigeria. A decade ago, I visited a northern community devastated by flooding. The U.S. and Nigerian Government built 400 free houses for the community. When I went to visit the houses, I saw northern kids wearing Osama bin Laden hats. So it is shocking for me to hear U.S. diplomacy that extremism is Nigeria driven by local factors, when clearly there is a tie-in to global jihad and even to U.S. policy.

Let me mention that while Egypt is America's most strategic geopolitical partner in North Africa, Nigeria is its foremost ally in sub-Saharan Africa. Nigeria has consistently brokered peace deals and rolled back coups in Africa. While Egypt's stabilization is aid-based and predicated on a balancing act, Nigeria's regional security role is largely self-propelled.

So for a partner such as this that the U.S. relies on to be boots on the ground in northern Mali, in Liberia, and so on and so forth, is somewhat disconcerting for the U.S. to be so critical of the Nigerian military. True, there are human rights abuses and I, as someone who was detained and tortured by the Nigerian Army during the rule of General Abacha, would not be the first person to speak on their behalf. But the fact of the matter is that if there was no state of emergency and if the troops did not go in, what is happening in Nigeria now would be far worse than what Boko Haram did last year.

Because many churches have been closed down and because the Nigerian Government is protecting a lot of these areas, here is what Boko Haram did in September while I was in Nigeria the week that you arrived, a few days before you arrived. They blocked a highway and they began to kill people from car to car. They killed about 170 people that day. Here is what Boko Haram did. They asked them their names and they used their ID cards to ensure that their names tallied with the names they gave. So that if you gave a Muslim name and they checked your ID card and it wasn't a Muslim name, they would identify you as a Christian and kill you. They killed 152 Christians that day. They used chain saws to behead people. Now it was not only Christians they killed. There were about 19 Muslims who had government-issued ID cards. So if you worked for a local government or a state government or authority or security operatives you would also be killed if you were a Muslim. The few Muslims who did not have ID cards, they were abducted by Boko Haram and taken away. We rescued a woman who escaped from a Boko Haram camp and I was curious why are they abducting these people and she told us that the Muslim abductees are taken to the camps and then they are trained and forcefully conscripted to become terrorists.

I say this to say that it is clear therefore that there are many Muslims who are not supportive or sympathetic to Boko Haram, but they are being intimidated by the terrorist antics of this group. We all know the truism that all it takes for evil to triumph is for good men to do nothing. And we have today come to a point where the U.S. has finally decided to do something.

I want to point out that there are some fighters of Boko Haram who are incentivized by two things. They were given transport money, as little as $30, to go and undertake jihad and they went to a church and they killed people, but they were always told that you are doing the work of Allah. So we see clearly a pattern that there are people who will take that little bribe to go out and do jihad. But then there are other people who are not interested in the bribe, but who are abducted and taken to those camps and made into terrorists. This story illustrates to my mind that it is not economics that is driving this. It is a warped theology.

And so when the administration implies that somehow it is the actions of the government that is causing this, it is highly misleading. I will point out that the north has been backward for a very long time, even under British colonial rule. So it is not overnight that you can pin it down to the current administration. Let me say that what is worrisome to me as an individual is that when 9/11 occurred, the whole world with one voice said this is unconscionable. Even in Iran, people protested and held vigils in sympathy with the United States. No one wanted to ask whether the U.S. fueled that situation by supporting bin Laden many years ago. That was not the time to ask that kind of question. We recognized evil for what it was and we stood up as one race to denounce it.

And then in Nigeria, terrorists do these atrocious deeds and all of a sudden we begin to psychoanalyze and say oh, this must be because of poverty. As you said so eloquently last time, that is an insult to poor people. There is no legitimate grievance on the planet that would encourage anyone to take a chain saw and cut off the head of an innocent person who is struggling to go on and make a phone call to his mother because he couldn't get a phone call signal in his state. And this is why it is my hope that as the U.S. cooperates with Nigeria more, they will encourage the Nigerian authorities to switch back the telecommunication systems in Borno State.

Let me just say that there is still a little work to be done. We have talked about the humanitarian assistance. The U.S. is spending a lot of money on interfaith dialogue when this is not an interfaith issue. This is a radicalization issue and we should be looking at either of two things, either a de-radicalization program for these people who are killing Christians as well as Muslims who are critical of them, or we should be looking at humanitarian assistance for victims so that desperate people do not feel the need to fight back.

I will also mention at this time that it is important for technical assistance for the Nigerian military because the U.S. has been down the same path that Nigeria is now going down, fighting an insurgency in Afghanistan. Boko Haram is modeled after the Taliban and I believe that there are lots of lessons learned that the United States can share with the Nigerian Army.

So as I said, they took the wind out of my sails. There is not very much more I can say. I will say in conclusion that this is not about a threat to America. The threat has gone beyond the mere threat. I was in Abuja the day that Boko Haram bombed the United Nations building and my friend, an American lawyer, was in that building when it was bombed. When it occurred, I phoned her because I was a meant to be in that building that day. And I hear my friend coughing in the smoke-filled building. She had not yet been rescued. To this day I have not heard one word from the United States Embassy about my friend who was in that building.

In addition to that, I later on learned that there was an American diplomat in that building when it was bombed. And so it concerns me that this is not a theoretical issue. This is practical. Boko Haram has killed people from Italy, from Germany, from France, and other numerous locations, about 15 countries at last count. Is it simply because my friend did not die that day that it has taken us so long to recognize Boko Haram as an FTO.

I thank you very much for inviting me to speak to you today. Thank you.

[The prepared statement of Mr. Ogebe follows:]

Testimony of Mr. Emmanuel Ogebe, Esq.

On Behalf of the Jubilee Campaign

On

The Rising Global Threat of Boko Haram& US Policy Intransigence

Before the

Subcommittee on Africa, Global Health, Global Human Rights, and International Organizations

and the

Subcommittee on Terrorism, Nonproliferation, and Trade

Subcommittee on Africa, Global Health, Global Human Rights, and International Organizations

Rep. Christopher H. Smith, Chairman

Subcommittee on Terrorism, Non-proliferation and Trade

Rep. Ted Poe, Chairman

November 13, 2013

U.S. House of Representatives Foreign Affairs Committee

Mr. Chairmen, Ranking Members and Members of the Subcommittees: Thank you for the opportunity of allowing me to testify before you today.

I especially want to thank Chairman Smith for his outstanding leadership on this issue and for traveling to Nigeria to further investigate the situation, where he called for the Nigerian government to create a Boko Haram victim's compensation fund. Today, I would like to share five critical points concerning the unfolding situation in Nigeria.

I. Profiles Of Terror

The People for the Propagation of the Prophet's teaching, also known as Boko Haram was recently described as "one of the most vicious terrorist organizations in the world" by President Obama. The Nigerian-based Jihadist group was ranked the 2nd deadliest terrorist group worldwide – after the Taliban – by the State Department's 2012 US Terrorism report.

Boko Haram emerged around 2002 as a self-styled "Nigerian Taliban" in direct response to the US invasion of Afghanistan and the dislodgment of the Taliban[1]. Since its first attack against Nigerian police stations, interestingly, on Christmas Eve 2003, Boko Haram has evolved into a lethal terror group after its role model in just a decade.

From the time it issued an ultimatum, shortly after blowing up churches on Christmas day, asking Christians and southerners to leave Northern Nigeria in January 2012 or die, Boko Haram has prosecuted a pernicious and systematic campaign of extermination. Funerals for randomly killed non-Muslim "others" havebeen attacked, companies have been raided, and non-Muslims summarily executed by shots to the head, buses have been stopped with the occupants separated and systematically slaughtered. More Christians

---

[1]Onmonya, George, *Boko Haram and History*, http://nigeriavillagesquare.com/guest-articles/boko-haram-and-history.html

were killed in northern Nigeria in 2012 than throughout the rest of the world[2]. Despite a state of emergency meant to rout out the insurgents after they captured significant swathes of territory in Nigeria's northeast, military sources say they have only liberated about 75% of territory previously lost to Boko Haram. In a recent trip to an insurgent strong-hold, it was clear that Boko Haram is operating unfettered in the mountain ranges of Gwoza. Three churches and 21 homes were burnt and the father of one of our interviewees was killed just miles away from our hotel. These incidents barely made it into the local news. September marked the highest death toll since 2009 with deaths in the region of 500 including a rush hour ambush in which chainsaws were used to decapitate travelers, a school massacre, a military ambush and scorched earth raids on villages in Gwoza. Like Tora Bora, the hills of Gwoza have become a bastion of insurgency. In fact there is a region in Yobe actually renamed "Kandahar" by the terrorists.

This year, there has been a sustained level in the number of church attacks inspite of the increased security. In 2012, about 47 churches were attacked. This year 53 churches have already been attacked and 216 people murdered in them. Last year, there were two attacks on mosques carried out by Boko Haram resulting in 19 deaths and this year there have already been two attacks, with an increased death rate of 52, indicating an upward trend in the severity of such attacks.

Inspite of the well documented nexus with global jihad that goes as far back as Nigerian Islamist fighters being captured fighting alongside the Taliban during the US invasion of Afghanistan, and Bin Laden's personal secretary admitting to traveling to Nigeria in a New York court, the US continues to discount the full global antecedents and intents of Boko Haram.

---

[2]World Watch Monitor, *Widest Church Groupings Raises Funds for Boko Haram's almost 800 Victims in 2012*, March 8, 2013,
http://www.worldwatchmonitor.org/2013/03-March/2331194/

So while the President is on point in his description of Boko Haram as one of the most vicious terrorist organizations in the world, his administration's response has been anything but precise.

II. A Deadly Misdiagnosis: How The U.S. Has Framed The Issue Improperly

Part of the State Department's response has been to deny the religious motivation of a rabid jihadist group that has repeatedly declared its goal of overthrowing the state and establishing a radical Muslim theocracy; to downplay the repeated threats to America going back several years by claiming this is all "local"; presenting arguments rationalizing terrorism by psycho-analyzing the emotional disconnect between the central government and northern Muslims who fuel the terrorism; pressing the government to throw money at the problem with no emphasis on victim compensation, and being more critical of the military counteroffensive than of the terrorists' atrocities.

This has led to an absurd situation where the terror group has had to clarify its jihadist credentials in almost direct rebuttals of State Department characterizations. When the US said Boko Haram is "not religious" but economically motivated, the terrorists invested in a video to correct this misinformation. In a video released last week on November 3rd, Boko Haram leader Shekau claimed responsibility for the deaths of 35 people on an October 24 attack in the northern city of Damaturu. He stated: "This is a brief message to the world. We carried out the Damaturu attacks with Allah's help, with Allah's might, with Allah's glory and with victory from Allah, the Creator."[3] Shekau and his group are not shy about the fact that they kill in the name of their Creator. In regard to the FTO designation, BokoHaram is substantially ahead of the US – they have long since assumed that they have already been designated and they have designated the US a Foreign Target Objective!

---

[3] http://news.yahoo.com/boko-haram-video-claims-october-24-attack-killed-185857285.html

A decade ago I visited a Nigerian community devastated by flooding. The US and Nigerian governments built 400 free houses for them. When I went to the houses, I saw northern children wearing Osama bin Laden hats. What was shocking to me is that US diplomats are aware of the intense anti-American sentiments in northern Nigeria but somehow the US misrepresents this as being "local".

But beyond the farcical elements of State's misinterpretations of Boko Haram's clear message and intent, there are more troubling assertions that could portend great harm to America's biggest ally in sub-Saharan Africa.

First, the Department of State asserts that the north feels distanced from the central government headed by President Jonathan and has been politically marginalized. This statement was made less than one year after he was elected. Could the president in office forless than 1 year be responsible for the neglect of the north, which has occupied the presidency for 70% of the nation's history? How would State explain the riots in 12 states that destroyed over 500 churches, which occurred even before President Jonathan's electoral victory was announced? The fact remains that the backwardness of the north is a reality that dates back to British colonial rule and one that cannot now be reassigned vicariously to Nigeria's Federal government.

State's proposed solution was for Nigeria to give more money and positions to the Muslim north which it specifically distinguished from central Nigeria which is majority Christian and especially to cuddle "Hausa Fulani" leaders.

Here is the reality: The north already has the majority of top government positions including 80% of the most senior positions – Senate President, House Speaker, Chief Justice and Vice President. Only the President is not from the north.

But in its tribalist-based assessment of the situation in Northern Nigeria, State singled out the Hausa Fulani for rapprochement whereas the hub of the insurgency is the Kanuri tribe in the northeast. In fact, the Hausa Fulani are not only considered to have oppressed minorities in the north but also the rest of the country as well! How did the Department of State miss it so badly on a simple cultural and historic fact? This is as bad as saying the Redskins should apologize for using that name - to the British.

Even worse is the US prescription for more money to the north in furtherance of the sophist argument that this is "economic". By reinterpreting the jihadist movement in its own image State has succeeded in negotiating a ransom on behalf of terrorists demanding "protection money" from the federal government in violation of all the principles of federalism. The Federal government of Nigeria does more for its individual states than the US government does for its states, providing generally 80% of many states' budgets.[4]

The ultimate danger here is that the US is opening a slippery slope to the institutionalization of mass murder as a legitimate pathway to more federal resources. This could create a precedent that if you blow up churches, the US will advocate on your behalf (not on behalf of victims) to earn you a federal ministry. The end result would be horrendous - different segments of the 360+ tribes who have "legitimate grievances" will seize upon terrorism as the way forward and Nigeria will know no peace ever again! The rule of law will be completely eviscerated.

On Easter Monday last year at a CSIS event in Washington, DC the top US diplomat for Africa then, Ambassador Johnnie Carson declared, "I want to stress that religion does not drive extremism in Jos or northern Nigeria" despite the fact that 38 innocent Nigerians were killed in terrorist bombings the day before during Easter celebrations and despite the fact that Boko Haram has attacked Christians hundreds of times. His solution: "(The Government of Nigeria) will have to develop an economic recovery strategy that compliments its security strategy...The Nigerian government should consider creating a Ministry of Northern Affairs or a development commission."

---

[4] Niaraland.com Forum, *Internally Generated Revenue- Lagos, Sokoto Lead the Way*, July 23, 2009, http://www.nairaland.com/300410/nigeria-igr-internally-generated-revenue

To state that religion does not play a role in the extremism exhibited by the terrorist group is disingenuous at best and deeply insensitive to victims. To propose that it can be fixed with a commission is naïve. The US sent out billions in cash that was physically distributed around Iraq, but still signally failed to win hearts and minds to stem insurgency. To propose a repeat methodology and expect different results certainly meets Einstein's threshold of insanity.

America's missed opportunity in properly understanding and promptly responding to the Boko Haram threat has misled the Government of Nigeria, weakened its response and resulted in numerous lives lost plus a heightened and highly evolved threat to the US homeland and global community.

If after September 11th, the global community had responded by pontificating on America's perceived sins to the Arab world instead of rallying around to jointly disavow terrorism, giant strides would not have been made in decimating Al Qaeda. This is why the US response to a crucial African ally is unfair and unfortunate.

Questions still arise – what happened to the Nigerian foreign fighters found fighting alongside Al Qaeda and the Taliban in Afghanistan when NATO troops invaded in 2001? They did not go to Gitmo so were they released to return to Nigeria and start the Nigerian Taliban? The intelligence gaps here are deep and wide…Regardless of what happened a dozen years ago, the intelligence lapses now are of the utmost concern. Last year, the formerAmbassador Johnnie Carson dissimulated before this committee on a simple question: whether there were Iranian arms in Nigeria – a matter that was before the UN Security Council and had been reported in numerous media. He claimed ignorance.

This was inspite of the fact that in violation of UN sanctions requested by the United States, Iran had surreptitiously shipped 13 containers of weapons into Nigeria, which the Nigerian government confiscated and reported to the UN Security Council. As a colleague stated: even if Ambassador Carson's defense is that he has not been reading cables from the US embassy in Nigeria, what is his excuse for not reading the Washington Post? The Iran arms story appears in the most elementary Google search.

Those rocket-propelled grenadeswere reportedly linked to staff of the Iranian embassy in Abuja, Nigeria. The Iranian Foreign Minister flew into Nigeria and, invoking diplomatic immunity, rescued a suspected Iranian official from hiding in the embassy and flew him home.

Here is where it gets interesting. The Nigerian government, embarrassed and miffed by this total violation of diplomatic norms, reported this arms shipment to the United Nation's Security Council as a violation of resolutions and sanctions sought for and obtained by the US against Iran.

When Ambassador Carson denied knowledge of arms shipments from Iran to Nigeria, it simply was incredible for the top diplomat for Africa, and a former intelligence officer at that, to claim not to know of a serious international incident rising to the level of the UN Security Council on an issue driven by the US.

In the wake of the attacks of September 11th, Nigeria's then president Obasanjo flew to Washington to condole with President Bush. A dozen years later, President Obama avoided Nigeria, its biggest trading partner in the continent, on his second Africa trip reportedly citing abuses by the security forces.

III.   US Actions and Inactions

The US has lagged behind in humanitarian assistance. It hasnot providedanything to victims of the Boko Haram terrorism crisis. Even less still is said to the Federal Government about providing victim assistance. Nigeria's President announced last week that he would not provide compensation for victims.

USAID has a PEACE project that researches extremism in target countries. Inspite of the data that puts Nigeria at the front of terror activity, USAID has not made Nigeria a priority country. In fact, in its bidding documents, it lists Nigeria specifically as an example of a country that doesn't suffer extremism, but does not make an effort to study the situation to prove or disprove its assumption.

The US has presented an award to a hardline Muslim Imam who would not let American officials into his mosque. At the same time, it has labeled Christian ministers whose congregants are being slaughtered in the thousands as "radical", which is ironic given the manner civil rights pastors were marked in America's own history.

In regards to regional security cooperation, the US looked beyond the oil producing region to include northern Nigeria in its Bi-national Commission. However, where it donated a ship to the Nigerian Navy years ago for the NigerDelta, there islittle technical assistance against the Boko Haram terrorism. At the time a Nigerian policeman died while detonating bombs with his bare hands, there is talk of US providing bomb detonation robots - a full two years after bombings began. Interestingly, the US rushed to provide bomb detectors in Nigerian airports after the failed airplane bombing by a Nigerian AQIM operative Abdul Mutallab.

On intelligence cooperation, it is unclear what is occurring.President Obama reportedly cancelled his Nigeria visit on account of satellite pictures showing a major gun battle in the fishing hamlet of Baga. If the US had access to such satellite images, why didn't they alert the Nigerian authorities to the fact that Boko Haram had captured significant amounts of territory and was flying its flag in several captured counties?

In the same vein, while the US was working to contain the spread of post-Qaddafi arms in Libya and recovered 800 out of 5000 missing missiles, not much was done to contain their influx into Nigeria since 2011. Sadly, history repeated itself when arms from northern Mali once again flowed into northern Nigeria following the US-backed, French-led and Nigeria-supported counteroffensive against the jihadists. Although the US consul general did raise public concern, it is unclear if strategic containment mechanisms were initiated.

One historic footnote that deserves mention is that even the Niger Delta militancy that threatened US oil supplies and shot up global oil prices was a direct product of Libyan state-sponsored terrorism - financing, arming and Mujaheed training. Again, a terror export to Nigeria that somehow fell through the cracks.

The most worrisome aspect of US action is the announcement of a new consulate in northern Nigeria. Carson indicated that the US is opening a consulate in Kano to achieve closer ties with the region. The problem is that the US embassy in Abuja is not allowing ANY American officials travel outside the capital due to fear of attack. It routinely issues advisories to American visitors that the cities' prominent hotels are under threats for being "western." Isn't it a brilliant idea to place more American lives and property at great expense in grave danger at the height of a low-grade insurgency that claimed more lives in one day than in either Iraq, Afghanistan or Pakistan in 2012? On January 20, 2012 Boko Haram went on a large scale onslaught against security agencies in the northern Nigerian city of Kano. The police headquarters, barracks, intelligence headquarters and police stations were amongst the numerous targets of simultaneous attacks that left over 200 people dead. It was to be the highest single day death toll in any global conflict in 2012 until Syria tied with Kano much later in the year.

Three months later in April, 2012, Johnnie Carson declared that the US was going to open a consulate in Kano and that the State Department had "pots of money" ready to recruit Americans to go there. This was in a city where the police had shuttered several of their police stations after the January 20 siege because they could not defend their own stations, let alone the US consulate.

IV.   Foreign Terrorist Organization Designation

Finally, the US has not designated Boko Haram an FTO. This tool which would enable tracing and freezing of terror financing and potentially arms has been steadfastly squirreled away in a lockbox and the key thrown away. TheUS has designated Shekau and two other men associated with Boko Haram as terrorists. This year, in another classic non-starter, it went ahead to offer a $7 million bounty for the capture of Abu Shekau. Here is the problem – capturing the head without destroying the terrorists organization is not a winning strategy.Former Boko Haram leader Mohammad Yusuf was replaced by Shekau. More importantly, even the multi-million dollar Bin Laden bounty did not result in his capture. It was old-fashioned, dogged police work plus Special Forces that got the job done.

According to the U.S. Department of State, "FTO designations play a critical role in our fight against terrorism and are an effective means of curtailing support for terrorist activities and pressuring groups to get out of the terrorism business."[5] The U.S. has designated three Boko Haram radicals as terrorists, and the group's financing has been traced to groups that have already been designated FTOs by the United States.

In addition to being linked to Al-Qaeda in the Islamic Maghreb, Boko Haram's funding has been traced to other Al-Qaeda linked organizations in the Middle East.[6] Some of these other organizations include: the Islamic World Society (with headquarters in Saudi Arabia), and Al-Muntada Trust Fund (a Britain based organization).[7] Boko Haram's worldwide sources of funding demonstrate that the group is more than a ragtag bunch of Nigerians. In fact, Shekau has boasted that his group is now strong enough to "comfortably confront" the United States.[8]

Doesn't it seem strange that there has been an incredible amount of hesitation to designate Boko Haram as an FTO when Boko Haram itself has labeled the US a Foreign

---

[5] http://www.state.gov/j/ct/rls/other/des/123085.htm

[6] http://allafrica.com/stories/201202141514.html

[7] Id. and http://www.upi.com/Top_News/World-News/2012/02/13/Investigators-track-Boko-Haram-funding/UPI-25221329148725/

[8] http://cnsnews.com/news/article/nigerian-terror-group-boko-haram-designates-us-terror-target

Target Objective? In fact, Boko Haram meets the criteria for the FTO designation in accordance with section 219 of the Immigration and Nationality Act. The criteria are as follows: 1) The organization must be foreign based. 2) The organization engages in terrorist activity or terrorism, or retains the capability and intent to engage in terrorist activity or terrorism. 3) The terrorist activity or terrorism of the organization threatens the security of United States nationals or national security of the United States.[9]

Let me take a moment to expound on the third point. Boko Haram has attacked US nationals. I repeat - Boko Haram has attacked US citizens. During the bombing of the UN HQ in Abuja, there were several Americans known to be in the building who survived the attack. One was an American official stationed at the US embassy in Nigeria and the second was an American civilian working for the UN whom I was supposed to see at the UN that day. I was in Nigeria on the day of the bombing. Yet the U.S. has made no public statement about the survivors of that horrific attack. **Since then, Boko Haram has attempted to abduct an American in northern Nigeria.**

In conclusion, please permit me to juxtapose two geopolitical giants on the African continent. While one can understand the reluctance to recognize what happened in Egypt as a coup for fear of imposing sanctions by cutting aid to its topmost north African ally, how does one rationalize the reluctance to designate terrorism that would impose sanctions restricting terror financing to a vicious organization fighting the USA's topmost sub-Saharan ally?

Nigeria is doubtlessly a strategic security partner in the region and on the globe, and currently participates in 9 UN peacekeeping operations worldwide. The US has no troops in UN Peacekeeping operations since Somalia's Black Hawk down incident while Nigerian troops are currently in Somalia. Historically, the Nigerian army has paid considerably in lives and billions of dollars to end the war in Liberia – America's African child. Even this year, Nigerian troops joined the French army in dislodging Taureg

---

[9]http://www.state.gov/r/pa/prs/ps/2010/09/146554.htm

jihadists who took over northern Mali, while America stayed safely away by providing only limited logistic support. It is not a stretch to say that Nigeria has had boots on the ground in numerous situations of strategic interest to the US where the US could not or would not.

The Nigerian army does not receive up to one tenth of aid that the United States provides to the Egyptian army. However, Nigeria's army has done more for continental security, global peacekeeping and directly protecting US strategic interests than the Egyptian army. Is this the way to treat a strategic ally and regional stabilizer?

Terrorism in Northern Nigeria negatively affects the sub region as a whole. Chad, Niger and Cameroun are reeling from the influx of refugees and cross border infiltration.

Further, Nigeria is the 6th largest supplier of oil to the United States. 40 percent of its oil supply, or 281,291,000 barrels per year are exported to the United States. [10] The instability of Nigeria would undoubtedly have a negative effect on the amount of oil it produces and ships to the United States. Such a decrease in oil supply would be considerable if the former Niger Delta militancy was anything to go by, with potential consequences ranging from a drastic increase in gas prices, to a more vulnerable United States in regard to national security.

Essentially, the body language of the administration seems to hint - Boko Haram is your problem, not ours. This is well illustrated by the recent extradition from Nigeria to the US for trial of a Nigerian who acted as a translator/recruiter for another terrorist organization AQAP which has been designated an FTO[11]. Meanwhile chainsaw-wielding, suicide-bombing terrorists have not been labelled terrorists? This mentality is dangerous, and it is

[10]http://www.globalpost.com/dispatch/100726/top-7-us-oil-importers

[11]http://www.fbi.gov/newyork/press-releases/2013/alleged-international-terrorist-arraigned-today-in-brooklyn-federal-court-following-extradition-from-nigeria

my hope that the U.S. policy will be modified as soon as possible in order to adequately deal with Boko Haram - the vicious terrorist organization.

V. CONCLUSION

If the fundamental step of any 12-step recovery program is admitting there is a problem, then the US is stuck on ground zero. It concedes there is a problem but has enrolled in Alcoholics Anonymous instead of a Jihad Unanimous rehab group. The resulting prescriptions are bound to have contraindications from misdiagnosis.

Hopefully we are at the cusp of a new dawn following personnel changes at State that may well usher in a new policy. When State argued that designating Boko Haram would give it global street cred, Boko Haram was 5th on global terrorism indices. This year, it is second. This rise has occurred without the boost of an FTO designation.

To its credit, the Secretary Kerry's State Department has issued a $7 million bounty for the capture of Abu Shekau, Boko Haram's blood-thirsty Osama wanna be. But aside from the proven ineffectual nature of this approach to the classic decade-long pursuit of Bin laden, this match.com strategy for combatting terrorism is clearly a long shot in the dark. The US needs to move from retail piece-meal designation of favorite terrorists to wholesale designation of the entire organization. Half-hearted and half-baked measures are exactly how a Nigerian suicide bomber got on a flight to Detroit with a bomb in his underpants on Christmas Eve 2009 even though his father had walked into the American embassy and warned them about his son.

Chairman Smith is the lead sponsor of H.R. 3209, the Boko Haram Terrorist Designation Act of 2013. I strongly urge members of Congress of both parties to actively support the enactment of H.R. 3209. This does not need to be a partisan issue or a polarizing issue. This is a basic human rights issue. On behalf of many victims and their families, thank you, Chairman Smith, for your uncommon and unwavering care and concern for our common humanity.

Mrs. Deborah is carried to her son's casket. Boko Haram killed her husband and then abducted her two daughters ages 9 and 7. A few months later, they returned to her home and asked why she still hadn't converted. They then killed her son and his friend a fellow Boys' Scout.

Mr. SMITH. Mr. Ogebe, thank you very much for your testimony, your extraordinary leadership because I think you have been a consistent voice and certainly have been helpful to this subcommittee for years, so I do thank you for that and for the stories that you have recounted just a moment ago.

Mr. OGEBE. If I may, sir, I submit my written testimony for the record.

Mr. SMITH. Without objection, it will and any information you would like to attach to it, documents of whatever kind will be made a part of the record.

Mr. Adamu, please proceed.

STATEMENT OF MR. HABILA ADAMU, SURVIVOR OF VIOLENCE BY BOKO HARAM

Mr. ADAMU. Chairman Smith, Members of the Congress, it is a great opportunity for me to be here to testify on behalf of all wounded Christians, persecuted Christians, widows, and orphans of Nigeria.

My name is Habila Adamu. I am from Yobe, in the northern part of Nigeria. On 28 November, gunmen came to my house around 11 p.m. and confronted me with my family. I thought they were Nigerian Army patrol. When I opened the door of my sitting room, I am shocked when I see them. I went back. Now my wife moved forward in order to beg them not to kill me, to leave me a life. She offered them money. They collected the money and our cell phones. The leader told my wife that they are there to do the work of Allah. When I heard that, I know that that day I would see my Lord. I prayed a short prayer. I said, "Lord, I am a sinner. Here I am. I cannot save myself. Lord, forgive me. I write my name in the Book of Life. Save my soul, Lord." When I prayed, I move forward because they were there for me. The leader asked me "Habila, can we get the key of the door" because I am in my sitting room. I gave them the key of the main door. They opened the door. I know two people came inside, making four into my home, with AK–47s.

They asked my name and I told them, Habila Adamu. They asked me are you in the Nigerian Army? I said no. Are you a Nigerian police? I said no. Are you an SSS? I said no. I am a businessman. Because if I told them I am working with the government they would have slaughtered me like a lamb. I told them that I am a businessman. They said are you a Christian? I said yes, I am a Christian. They asked me why are we preaching the message of Mohammed and you refuse to accept Islam religion? And I told them I am a Christian. We are also preaching the message and the good news to those that do not know God and to you.

He told me, "Habila, do you mean that you Christians know God?" I said, "Yes, we know God. That is what I am preaching to you." He called my wife. He said, "Let her witness what will happen to her husband." He said, "Habila, you can deny your faith in order to be saved and live a good life." And I told him that "No, I am a Christian. I would rather die as a Christian." He told my wife, "Plead with your husband that you will live a good life." And I told him, "I am a Christian." He said, "I will give you last chance, deny your faith, Habila or are you ready to die as a Christian?" I told him, "I am ready to die as a Christian." Before I closed my mouth one of them fired at me with an AK–47. It passed through my nose. This is the entering place of the bullet, an AK–47. This is the exit place of the bullet, an AK–47. I fell down on my face, blood is rushing everywhere. One of them followed me, stepped on me two times to confirm whether I am still alive or I am dead. They have found out I am dead. They shout, ''Allah Akbar'' means Allah is great. They went out.

Even my wife thought that I am dead. She is crying, saying many things. She said, ''Lord, why? Why did you let these things happen? Why you leave my husband to die at this moment? I have little ones. What I can tell them about their father?'' She said, ''Lord, I thank you because I am aware my husband is inside of you. Lord, give me the heart to stand in the end and help my children to stand in their faith.'' When I heard that I said, ''Oh, I am still in the world. Lord, why me?''

Now because I won't want to have to sin against God I raised my head and told her I am still alive. I did not die. She is shocked. She said the way you are bleeding you will not survive. And I told her that even though I will not survive, I have a message to everyone that will hear my story when I leave this world. Please send this message that to live in this world is to live for Christ, to die is a gain.

For a few minutes tense everywhere. I asked her to go out and look for help, somebody to help me. All the Christians around, they were killed that night. I am the only survivor. From 11 o'clock until 7 a.m., my face was swollen, my eyes were closed. I am still alive. Many Christians that remain in Potiskum, each one will touch me and would cry, they said, ''Habila, until we meet in heaven, no one must die who will survive.'' I asked myself, why me? I said, Lord, why me, take my life, Lord. He keeps me for a reason.

I am pleading, Americans, I am pleading, I am crying on behalf of all wounded Christians and past dead Christians in Nigeria. Let this killing of innocent people stop. Let Nigeria hear the cry of the widows and the orphans to pay for their school fees, to pay for their feeding and also pay for the wounded soldiers. Let them rebuild the broken churches and the houses. I also take this opportunity to appreciate what the Voice of Christian Martyrs does to me. They have paid for my operation, they have paid for my housing, my feeding. The government did not stand for me, but they stand for me and Americans can stand for me. Thank you so much. Thank you very much.

[The prepared statement of Mr. Adamu follows:]

Congressional Testimony of Habila Adamu

On the Continuing Threat of Boko Haram

Before the House Subcommittee on Africa, Global Health, Global
Human Rights, and International Organizations

and the

Subcommittee on Terrorism, Non-proliferation and Trade

Committee on Foreign Affairs

U.S. House of Representatives

November 13, 2013

MY STORY

I Habila Adamu from Yobe state in Northern Nigeria. On November 28, 2012, gunmen came to my home at around 11:00 pm and confronted me with my family. I thought they were soldiers on patrol, and when they opened the door, I was shocked to see that they were wearing robes and masks.

The gunmen ordered me to come out with my family. And when I came out, they ordered my family to go back, and my wife begged them not to harm me. They said she should go back, because they were here to do the work of Allah.

When I heard that, I knew that they were here to kill me. And my wife brought money to them and begged them not to harm me, they collected the money and they also collected our cell phones. They asked me for the key of the door, and I gave it. One of them opened the door another two more people come inside, making them four in my house with Ak47.

They asked for my name and I told them, Habila Adamu. They asked if I am a member of Nigeria Police, I said no. Are you a Nigeria soldier? I said no. You are a member of the state security service (SSS), I said no, I told them that I am a business man.

"Okay, are you a Christian?" I said I am a Christian. They asked me why are we preaching the message of Mohammed to you and you refuse to accept Islam. I told them I am a Christian, we are also preaching the gospel of true God to you and other people that are not yet to know God. They asked me if I mean we Christian know God. And I told them we know God and that is why I preach the good news to other people that do not know God.

Then they asked me, "Habila, are you ready to die as a Christian?" I told them, "I am ready to die as a Christian." For the second time, they asked me, "Are you ready to die as a Christian?" and I told them, "I am ready," but before I closed my mouth, they have fired me through my noise (the entering point) and the bullet came out through the back. I fell on the ground. The gunmen thought I was already dead because they stomped on me two times and discovered I was dead, and cried out "Allah Akbar" (God is Great). Also my wife thought I was dead, she is crying, while crying she said many things, she said let God give her the heart that she can stand to the end like what I did, let God give my children the heart that they may stand in their faith. When she continues saying all those things, I told her that I am alive. She said that but even though you are alive, the way you are bleeding, you will not survive. And I told her that even though I will die I have a message to everyone that will hear my story after I leave this world that "to live in this world is to live for Christ, to die is a gain" that is my message. I asked her to look for help. And she went out; she found out that our Christian neighbors have been killed. We have one elder in my church, (Jibring Matinja) himself and his son were killed that night, including twelve others.

I was on the ground from 11:00 pm till 7:00am in the morning, bleeding. In the morning my face was swollen, my eyes were red. Before morning I could not see anything, around 7:00 am I was rushed to a hospital in Potiskum, for medication, from then they transferred me to Jos University Hospital (JUTH) same day. I am alive because God want you to have a message. I have a message, just as I told my wife as I was left for dead, I have a message to everyone that will hear my story. Do everything that you can to end this ruthless religious persecution in Northern Nigeria. My friends knowing Christ are deeper, than hearing of his name or knowing his story.

I also like to express my appreciation to God almighty and the Voice of Christian Martyrs for their supports, in standing by my side throughout, they paid for my operation, and paid for my housing, they paid for my feeding etc. Let God bless them abundantly.

Thank you!!!

He is the resurrection and the life, in the book of John 11:25 says "I am the resurrection and the life he who believe in me will live, even though he dies."

THE SUFFERINGS OF NIGERIA CHRISTIANS IN NORTHERN NIGERIA

Nigerian Christians had been under intense suppression and marginalization in the north for so many years, which has grown to the point where they are more like second class citizens in their own land of nativity without any one speaking for them or listening to their plight. This is reflected to the struggle they do have to normal education in the secondary school and tertiary institutions, in spite their resilience and hard work to studies which had been the bedrock of Christianity. Many of them who had read wide and far were denied employment opportunities and even when they were employed, they remained in one place for the rest of their lives. Worst of all is that, Christians with higher qualifications were forced to work under the supervisions of Muslims who had lower or less qualification. Most of the Northern State Government had established Ministries of religious affairs which cater only for the Islamic religion with all staff 100% Muslim staff without the consideration of the Christians. The Christians does not have the right to lands to build Churches where they will worship freely anymore. This subjugation and sabotage of their right and privileges had been ongoing for many years. In recent times, we saw expansion and occupation of the Muslims from the far north to the central part of Nigeria through calculated attacks on Christian communities in cities such as Jos, Kaduna, Kano, and Bauchi where several lives and hundreds of churches had been destroyed.

Most times these attacks are hidden under guise of provocation which made it to look like Christian and Muslim crisis. Many Nigerian stakeholders who are Muslim took side and kept suppressing the Christian and taking over their land and their houses without any complete and fulfilled investigations by the federal or state Governments. Because the perpetuators were not punished all the times these act of violence against the Christians kept continuing until now that it has grown to a level of total annihilation plan of the Christians in the North Using the so-called Boko haram terrorist group which had alliance with other international terrorist groups. The fundamentalist group had executed over 900 Christians in the last two years and over two thousand innocent Christians had died since 2009 when the group first attacks the Christian community in Maiduguri. These they do systematically with different methods of killings in different parts of the country. In The north Eastern part of Nigeria where Christian population is about 10% or less: They had been going towns to town's villages to villages and house to house of Christians and executing them in cold blood. Some Christians from those areas were killed in their business places and at the moment the Muslim's had comfortably taken over that business. They killed barbarically by gunshot, cutlass and machetes brutal killings while many were slaughtered like animals in their homes. They started with the killing of the Christian leaders, and Top Christian Civil servants in the Federal Governments and the few who had held some recognized offices in the state civil service and local Governments, then to every other Christians.

These kinds of killing were not in any way reported by the media; even when it is reported, they are always seen as one of those things, without any investigation, no indictment and no justice. At the moment most of the Christian and their Churches had been evacuated from those areas; especially Borno and Yobe states and for the few that are still living there who had nowhere to run to, They are like condemn criminals waiting for the day of their execution by the Islamic fundamentalist who seems to be unstoppable by the Nigeria government in their own mother land as though they are fugitives claiming the lives of over 340 Christians.

In places such as Bauchi State, with two Local Governments which are 95% Christians, the State Government itself had been terrorizing the Christian populace and given a brooding ground for the fundamentalists who had attacked over 35 villages killing over 280 Christians in the last two years. They attacked on their way to the state capital for businesses and other functions, on their farms while working and in their homes mostly in the night while sleeping. Many of the Christians had remained homeless and several of them had moved away from their villages as refugees in other parts of the neighbouring state.

These attacks continued in other North central states such as Plateau State and Kaduna state where several villages are being wiped out leaving several deaths and casualties which are always wrongly reported to seems as if it's a communal clash. These had claimed over 700 Christian lives in the last two years and over 50 villages in different parts of Plateau State had been completely destroyed and sent out of those locality. As if this is not enough, the group had attacked several churches and the Christians during church services in different parts of the North with one attacker being brought to book. These killings of Christians almost every day had clearly shows the commitment of the Islamic fundamentalists in establishing an Islamic state by total annihilation of Christians in the North. More than 350 Christians had died in these suicide bomb attacks.

THE RESULT OF ALL THE ATTACKS:

As result of all these attacks, the Christian community in Northern Nigeria had been left with the following predicaments:

➢ Lost of human dignity and subjugation to threats and fear with daily psychological trauma because of their faith.
➢ Daily increase of widows and orphans that kept becoming a fundamental burden on the Christian community.
➢ Lost of Churches and places of worship in Hundreds that denied them of the right to worship.
➢ Increase in the number of disable and disfigured Christians as a result of direct attack e.g. over 45 amputees with leg and hands amputations in Plateau State alone, 7 – 8 people with total and one eye blindness and several other disabilities and disfigurement.
➢ Over 240 Christians Villages deserted and over 5000 Christian's homeless.

———————

Mr. SMITH. Thank you so very much for that very powerful testimony. I would just note parenthetically that it was the Voice of Christian Martyrs and Pastor Richard Wurmbrand, his book, Tortured for Christ, as the book that got me in 1981 into the religious freedom issue. He was held by the Romanian Securitate, tortured almost to death several times, and then wrote a book when he finally got out about the persecuted Church which has been revolutionary in mobilizing people around the world to stand up for the persecuted Church. So thank you for being such a hero and for telling all of us that we need to do more. Thank you so very much.

Mr. ADAMU. Sir, I submit for the record, I submit my testimony for the record.

Mr. SMITH. Without objection, it will be made a part of the record.

Mr. Zenn, thank you, and welcome.

STATEMENT OF MR. JACOB ZENN, RESEARCH ANALYST, THE JAMESTOWN FOUNDATION

Mr. ZENN. Thank you very much, Chairman, for the opportunity to speak here. It is also an honor to be speaking next to these distinguished panelists, especially it is important that Mr. Adamu is here to provide a personal face to issues that can seem so far away to people here in America.

Part of my objective of being here today is to share some analysis on this group because only through strong analysis and understanding of where this group is operating, how it is funded, who are its members can we actually develop strategies to counter it beyond symbolic gestures.

I have, however, included some policy options for the U.S. in my written testimony and the Wall Street Journal article that was published yesterday called ''Boko Haram Isn't Only Nigeria's Problem.''

Now there are two main reasons why Boko Haram is not only Nigeria's problem. I would like to start by noting that in 2002, Boko Haram set up an Afghanistan compound modeled after the Taliban, two miles from the Niger border. After it engaged in clashes with the local community and security forces, its members fled across to the border to Niger. In 2004, Boko Haram organized its first attacks on the security forces in the Mandara Mountains between Nigeria and Cameroon, again its members fled into Cameroon after those attacks. In 2009, in July, there were for 4 days a series of attacks between Boko Haram and security forces. Thirty percent of Boko Haram members fled into the border region after those attacks, one member fled to Somalia and later masterminded the attacks on the U.N. headquarters in 2011. It is also after 2009 that Boko Haram went underground and it no longer solicited its funding sources from traditional mainstream sources. As a result, although the FTO label can help effectuate a crackdown on mainstream funding to Boko Haram, most of its funding is now local and informal. And therefore, it will require other measures and strategies at the more local level to counter Boko Haram funding.

In May 2013, the Nigeria security forces again launched an offensive against Boko Haram as part of a state of emergency, but again Boko Haram fled into the border region. Its leader, Abubakar

Shekau, who has a $7 million bounty on his head, has been reported in Mali, Niger, and Cameroon all in the past year. Until efficient border strategy is implemented to crack down on Boko Haram involving Nigeria and its French-speaking neighbors and including leadership from the U.S. and France, no matter what policies we take here in Washington or the Nigerian security forces take, Boko Haram cannot be defeated.

The U.S. should know, as well as any other country, how difficult it is to suppress an insurgency when the insurgents can go into a neighboring country and receive sanctuary. We have experienced this in Afghanistan. To give you an example, Algeria recently established 80 border posts in its country. That is an example of a country taking border security seriously. We need to see that type of collaboration in Nigeria.

The second reason why Boko Haram is not only Nigeria's problem is because of the breakaway faction Ansaru which is an al-Qaeda in the Islamic Maghreb extension in Nigeria. It is basically Nigerian members of al-Qaeda in Islamic Maghreb, who for the sake of efficiency have established an operation in Nigeria. I would submit, in fact, that the U.N. headquarters attack, the Federal Police headquarters attack, and the string of suicide bombings of churches in the middle belt of Nigeria in 2012 show the al-Qaeda in the Islamic Maghreb footprint more than the grassroots footprint of Boko Haram. Ansaru's leaders and founders, for example, Barnawi and Kambar, who have been designated by terrorists by the U.S. received their training in Algeria in the 2000s and even operated with Mokhtar Belmokhtar, a famed kidnapper in the Sahel as early as the 1990s.

The symbolism of Ansaru, which I have depicted in the written testimony, and its propaganda, are also consistent with al-Qaeda in the Islamic Maghreb and its attack style, kidnapping foreigners for kidnapping and ransom is also the same style as al-Qaeda in the Islamic Muslim in the Sahel. I would also submit that the French family that was kidnapped in Cameroon in February 2013, as well as the attack on a prison in Niamey, Niger in June 2013 to free Nigerian militants were also the work of Ansaru and international militant networks.

As a result, I think this FTO label must target specifically Ansaru and Jama'atu Ahlis Sunna Lidda'wati wal-Jihad which is actually the official name of the group that we call Boko Haram, based in the border region. Boko Haram has, however, become a nebulous term to refer to all types of violence in Nigeria so in order to effectuate this FTO label, let us focus it specifically on these two groups and use other non-securitized measures to tackle radicalization in Nigeria, which relates to land conflicts between majority ethnic Muslim groups and Christian groups, as well as the result of foreign support of radical groups and that includes countries like Iran, Saudi Arabia, that have supported the development of radical groups where Boko Haram also has its roots even in the 1990s and 2000s.

So thank you very much. I really appreciate the opportunity to speak here today.

[The prepared statement of Mr. Zenn follows:]

"The Continuing Threat of Boko Haram"
Testimony before the
Subcommittee on Africa, Global Health, Global Human Rights, and International
Organizations and Subcommittee on Terrorism, Nonproliferation, and Trade
November 13, 2013

Members of Congress, Ladies and Gentlemen:

My name is Jacob Zenn. I am a Research Analyst of African and Eurasian Affairs for The Jamestown Foundation. The views I express in this testimony are my own.

Thank you for inviting me to testify before you today on the topic of "The Continuing Threat of Boko Haram."

In this testimony, I will answer the following questions:

- How can the U.S. support Nigeria counter terrorist groups?
- Who is Boko Haram and who is Ansaru?
- Where do Boko Haram and Ansaru get their funding?
- Are Boko Haram and Ansaru connected to al-Qaeda?
- Do Boko Haram and Ansaru present a threat beyond Nigeria?

1. How can the U.S. support Nigeria counter terrorist groups?

Below are 10 measures the U.S. can take to support Nigerian counter-terrorism efforts:

- Develop a 'Marshall Plan' for northeastern Nigeria and use those funds to build schools, hospitals, infrastructure, water sources and recreational facilities, especially after army offensives clear out Boko Haram insurgents. The program would need to be transparent and have strong leadership to ensure projects are implemented.

- Label Boko Haram as a "foreign terrorist organization (FTO)," which could bring the power of international financial and anti-money laundering institutions to bear on Boko Haram's financial sponsors. Otherwise, this label is meaningless and should be abandoned; if Boko Haram is not an FTO, then who is?

- Mentor Nigerian troops in counter-insurgency based on best practices learned from years of dealing with IEDs, urban warfare and ambushes in Iraq and Afghanistan. Currently, the Leahy Act effectively bans U.S. support to Nigeria's Joint Task Force (JTF) that is fighting Boko Haram. Even JTF units with positive human rights records are blacklisted because of Leahy's wide-reaching ban on entire units— rather than specific abusers. Leahy should be reexamined, or else Nigeria will continue to look to countries like Pakistan for mentorship, which is no recipe for success.

- Formalize a sub-regional partnership between Nigeria and its French-speaking neighbors (Cameroon, Chad and Niger), where Boko Haram retreats after launching attacks in Nigeria. The U.S.-funded pan-Sahelian counter-terrorism initiatives are not tailored to deal with the unique drivers of the insurgency in Nigeria's borderlands, where Boko Haram and other criminal gangs have been left unchecked for too long. The U.S. should also seek French support in this initiative.

- Assist Nigeria to draft emergency laws with fast-track courts and specialist judges, prosecutors, defenders and investigators who can swiftly try cases of captured Boko Haram members. Wavering Boko Haram members who were forcibly conscripted may prefer prison to death at the hands of JTF, anti-Boko Haram civilian militias, or their own commanders, who kill and torture militants who disobey orders. U.S. lawyers who have experience in conflict resolution should partake in this initiative.

- Fund U.S. universities to teach Hausa, Fulani and other indigenous African languages. Only through sharper local source analysis can the U.S. enhance intelligence gathering on Boko Haram and other African militant groups and engage effectively with the civil society organizations to implement grassroots-driven programs to counter Boko Haram propaganda and recruitment.

- Recognize the distinct Borno-Yobe and ethnic Kanuri dimension of Boko Haram and incorporate local narratives to effectively counter Boko Haram's messaging and recruiting.

- Work with religious leaders and professionals to build skills and acquisition centers in northeastern Nigerian communities. This can be supported by community development funds, which provide support for small-medium business start-ups.

- Create strategies to combat one of the biggest problems the Nigerian government faces in containing Boko Haram and other Nigerian militant groups, which is that they have sympathizers in government that help them carry out "inside jobs."

- Partner with the Nigerian diaspora in the U.S. and UK and other countries to develop innovative and locally driven solutions to combat insurgent movements and corruption in Nigeria and promote accountability and transparency.

2. Who is "Boko Haram" and who is Ansaru?

"Boko Haram" refers to an Islamist group based in northeastern Nigeria. It was led by imam Mohammed Yusuf from 2002 to 2009. Yusuf's teachings differed from mainstream Islamist fundamentalist groups in Nigeria in two main ways: 1) he prohibited Western education; and 2) he prohibited service in the secular Nigeria government. In addition, he

believed the only "legitimate" Sunni Islamic states and scholars in the modern day are the Taliban, Usama bin Laden and al-Qaeda (particularly al-Qaeda in the Islamic Maghreb).

In July 2009, Yusuf's followers and the Nigerian government engaged in a four-day battle in northeastern Nigeria. The Nigerian security forces captured Yusuf at the house of a relative in Borno State's capital, Maiduguri, and executed him after interrogation at a police station. They also killed up to 1,000 of his followers during the clashes; about 20-30 security officials were also killed. Yusuf's execution – perceived as "martyrdom" – was recorded on a cell phone and is now widely available on YouTube and other websites.

In July 2010, Yusuf's former deputy Abubakar Shekau, who the security forces believed was killed in the July 2009 clashes, emerged as Boko Haram's new leader. He issued a video message "on behalf of my mujahideen brothers in some African territory called Nigeria... to the soldiers of Allah in the Islamic State of Iraq in particular," and warned that "Jihad has just begun... O America, die with your fury." Since Shekau took over the leadership, Boko Haram-related violence in Nigeria has been responsible for about 4,000 deaths in Nigeria.

Note: Shekau gave "Boko Haram" the name *Jama'atu Ahlis Sunna Lidda'awati wal-Jihad* (Sunni Group for Preaching and Jihad). No group in Nigeria actually calls itself Boko Haram, which means "Western education is sinful;" it is a nickname from locals and the media.

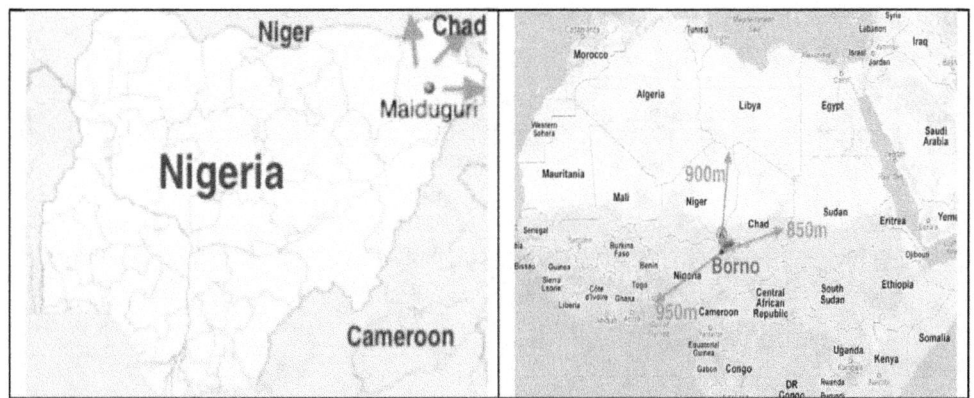

*Boko Haram is based in **Borno State**, Nigeria, whose capital, **Maiduguri**, is 100 miles from the **Cameroon, Chad and Niger** borders. Boko Haram has always been able to retreat, regroup and recruit in the border region before launching attacks in Nigeria. Boko Haram's base in Borno is also closer to **Sudan and Libya** than Lagos and is a former stopping point for West Africans on the way to hajj (pilgrimage) in **Mecca**, which is another reason why Boko Haram's connections to the **Sahel and Arab World** are closer than its connections within many parts of Nigeria. The Kanuris of Borno had "embassies" in modern-day **Tunisia** dating back to the 1300s and diplomatic relations with the **Ottoman Turks** in the 1700s— a time when Lagos and southern Nigeria were still largely unknown to the Kanuris.*

The JAMESTOWN
F O U N D A T I O N

Ansaru members are mostly Nigerians with militant origins dating back to their training in the Sahel (Mauritania, Algeria, Mali, Niger) in the late 1990s and early 2000s with militants who later formed al-Qaeda in the Islamic Maghreb (AQIM). Ansaru became active in Nigeria first under the under the name "al-Qaeda in the Lands Beyond the Sahel" in 2011, but in 2012 changed its name to Ansaru (*Jama'atu Ansaril Muslimina Fi Biladis Sudan*—the People for Supporting the Muslims in Black Africa). The name change may be attributed to al-Qaeda in the Islamic Maghreb (AQIM) leader Abdelmalek Droukdel's advice to Sahelian militants that it is "better for you to be silent and pretend to be a 'domestic' movement…There is no reason for you to show that we have an expansionary, jihadi, al-Qaeda or any other sort of project."

Ansaru, which the UK designated as a proscribed terrorist group in 2012, has been responsible for the following attacks, among others:

- Kidnapping and killing a British and Italian engineer of an Italian construction company in Sokoto in January 2012;

- Kidnapping and killing a German engineer in Kano in May 2012 (which was claimed by and carried out with AQIM);

- Attacking the Special Anti-Robbery Squad prison in Abuja in November 2012 and freeing dozens of prisoners;

- Kidnapping a Frenchman from the compound of an energy company near the border with Niger in Katsina State in December 2012 (he remains in captivity).

- Ambushing a convoy of three buses carrying 180 Nigerian soldiers through Okene, Kogi State, en route to Mali, killing two soldiers. Ansaru claimed the troops "were aiming to demolish the Islamic Empire of Mali" and warned African countries to "stop helping Western countries fight Muslims."

- Breaking into a prison and kidnapping and killing seven foreigners from a construction site in northeastern Nigeria's Bauchi State in February 2013.

- Ansaru was also likely responsible for the **UN Headquarters bombing** in Abuja on August 26, 2011 and the string of **suicide bombings of churches** in the Middle Belt in 2011 and 2012. Its members may also have participated in the **kidnapping of a seven-member French family in northern Cameroon** on February 19, 2013 (the family was released weeks later in exchange for $3 million and the release of Boko Haram members from Cameroonian prisons). Finally, its members participated in Mokhtar Belmokhar's attacks at the energy plant in **In Amenas, Algeria in Februrary 2013 and attacks in Arlit and Agadez, Niger in May 2013.**

One example of the AQIM-Ansaru connection is evidenced by their symbolism. The Algerian national emblem (left), the Salafist Group for Preaching and Combat logo (center), and Ansaru logo (right) all include a rising sun symbolizing a "new dawn." When a Boko Haram-Ansaru courier was arrested in 2012, he told the security forces that his funding came not from Boko Haram but from the "Group from the Sunset." The Salafist Group for Preaching and Combat was the predecessor to AQIM.

Similar to AQIM, Ansaru depicts itself in Sahelian attire (left), while Boko Haram, which is the more "Nigerian" group, depicts itself in green military fatigues similar to the U.S. and Nigerian militaries (right).

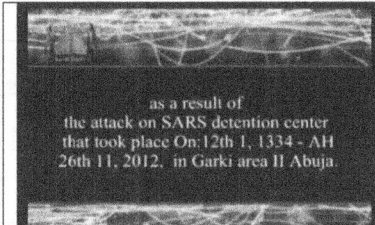 

An example of Ansaru's connections with the broader al-Qaeda movement is that in November 2012 its video claim (left) of a prison break in Abuja contained the exact same nasheed (Islamic music) as the Pakistan-based Islamic Movement of Uzbekistan's praise of jihads (right) in various theatres of Africa, including Nigeria. The nasheed is extremely rare and includes the chant "Ansar." In contrast, Boko Haram has frequently reached out to al-Qaeda, but al-Qaeda has not "endorsed" Boko Haram—likely because its killing of civilians would be a detriment to al-Qaeda's image. If the intelligence community fails to recognize Ansaru's international connections, it will inhibit operations against its networks in the future.

The JAMESTOWN FOUNDATION

3. Where do Boko Haram and Ansaru get their funding?

Before July 2009, Boko Haram received funding through Salafist and other Sunni Islamic organizations, such as those in Saudi Arabia, Sudan and Libya. Some of these organizations were likely connected to the UK. Boko Haram was also supported by Nigerian politicians, who wanted to curry favor with the group (since it was popular) and to benefit from "hiring" its rank-and-file *al-majiri* Islamic student members to carry out local vendettas on rivals. Such connections between politicians and Boko Haram likely still exist, but not as much as before July 2009. Since 2010, Boko Haram has also robbed dozens of banks in northern Nigeria and stolen cattle and other valuable items from locals in northern Nigeria. Ansaru and Boko Haram both have received significant funding from AQIM and kidnappings-for-ransom.

4. Are Boko Haram and Ansaru connected to al-Qaeda?

Yes, Ansaru is an extension of AQIM in Nigeria and is connected to the broader international al-Qaeda network. Boko Haram has benefitted from connections to AQIM and al-Shabaab for weapons procurement, safe havens and receiving training in the Sahel, although al-Qaeda has never declared it an affiliate. Boko Haram's killing of innocent civilians has likely alienated al-Qaeda, which already has a "public relations" problem of being perceived as killing too many innocent civilians; this is one reason why Ansaru formally announced that it broke away from Boko Haram in 2011.

5. Do Boko Haram and Ansaru present a threat beyond Nigeria?

Yes, they both can carry out attacks throughout West Africa. Ansaru has operated with AQIM from Algeria to Niger to Nigeria. Boko Haram, however, has confined its attacks to Nigeria 99% of the time, but uses bases in Niger, Cameroon and Chad to retreat, regroup and recruit. However, both organizations, especially Boko Haram, have not developed a sophisticated online "outreach strategy" to connect with potential sympathizers in the West. Moreover, the Nigerian diaspora is mostly Christian and unsympathetic to Boko Haram. The possibility of attacking the U.S. homeland is a mid-term to long-term threat and would require enhanced capabilities and connections for both groups. They are more likely to target U.S. interests and personnel in southern Nigeria as a next step before the U.S. homeland.

Sources consulted:
American Foreign Policy Council, World Almanac on Islamism, "Boko Haram", 2012 (http://almanac.afpc.org/boko-haram#); West Point CTC Sentinel, "Cooperation or Competition: Boko Haram and Ansaru After the Mali Intervention," March 27, 2013 (http://www.ctc.usma.edu/posts/cooperation-or-competition-boko-haram-and-ansaru-after-the-mali-intervention); Council on Foreign Relations, "Ansaru: Who Are They And Where Are They From?" July 1, 2013 (http://blogs.cfr.org/campbell/2013/07/01/ansaru-who-are-they/); Sahara Reporters, "How to End Boko Haram's Terror," Sahara Reporters, September 13, 2013 (http://www.youtube.com/watch?v=5VkVYyHmV4o).

The JAMESTOWN
F O U N D A T I O N

Biography:

Jacob Zenn is an expert on northern Nigerian security and consultant on countering violent extremism for U.S think-tanks and international organizations in Nigeria and Tajikistan. He is the author of "Northern Nigeria's Boko Haram: The Prize in Al-Qaeda's Africa Strategy," published by The Jamestown Foundation in 2012 and based on his fieldwork in Boko Haram's main area of operations in northern Nigeria, northern Cameroon, Chad, and southern Niger. Mr. Zenn also writes reports on Nigerian security for The Jamestown Foundation Terrorism Monitor, West Point Combating Terrorism Center and The Soufan Group and produces geospatial analysis products for visualization for Courage Services. He is also a subject matter expert on Nigeria for the Foreign Military Studies Office (FMSO).

In February 2013, Mr. Zenn provided testimony on Islamist militancy in Central Asia to the US Congress Subcommittee on Terrorism, Nonproliferation, and Trade. He also briefed the Cultural Knowledge Consortium of Department of Defense, Department of State Center for Strategic Counter-terrorism Communications, Canadian Security and Intelligence Services, and Royal United Services Institute on Nigerian security. Mr. Zenn's forthcoming publications examine Boko Haram's threat to the United States, Algeria-Nigerian jihadist networks, women in Boko Haram operations and propaganda, and a monograph on "Violent Extremism in Nigeria: A Practical Policy Guidance For Decision Makers."

Mr. Zenn speaks Arabic, Swahili, Chinese, Russian, French, Uighur and Spanish in addition to his native English, and he is studying Hausa. He holds a Juris Doctorate from Georgetown Law, where he earned the commendation of Global Law Scholar. His legal expertise focuses on international civil society law and best practices related to freedom of association, and he co-leads a USAID-funded law reform program in South Sudan. Since September 2013, he has also served as a policy adviser to the Nigeria-American Leadership Council, which works with the Nigerian diaspora, US government and think-tanks, and civic groups in Nigeria to counter radicalization and promote accountability.

contact: jacobzenn@gmail.com
residence: 2nd congressional district, 9th ward, Pennsylvania

Mr. SMITH. Thank you very much, Mr. Zenn for your analysis and for your myriad of recommendations. I think you make a number of very tangible suggestions to the State Department and to us, so thank you very much.

Mr. ZENN. Thank you very much. I would be glad to work on them.

Mr. SMITH. Our next witness is Dr. Guy Nzeribe. Thank you so much for being here. All of you, thank you for your patience after that long delay from the voting and the floor is yours.

STATEMENT OF GUY NKEM NZERIBE, PH.D., PARTNER, GUY NZERIBE ASSOCIATES

Mr. NZERIBE. Thank you very much, Mr. Chairman. Thank you, Chairman Smith, for the privilege and opportunity to testify before your joint subcommittees, as you begin the important deliberations and the critical issue of declaring Boko Haram a foreign terrorist organization. Thank you, Ranking Member Bass. I also thank you for the opportunity to come here and address these issues with you.

Many of my comments are based directly on my familiarity with the country, close observations with developments therein, and easy access to the political class in Nigeria.

As Chairman Smith and Chairman Poe have determined, Boko Haram is engaged in activities that terrorize the general Nigerian populace and with the allied Ansaru group, also foreigners. As such, Boko Haram has become part of a broader strategic challenge to the United States and our international partners.

Today, I want briefly to offer some context for this challenge, share what I have learned and suggest a view of Boko Haram that is increasingly being shared by analysts in Nigeria. I believe it is an extremely important area that has not received the attention it deserves from the intelligence and law enforcement communities. Of course, this approach does not override the determination of Boko Haram as a force for evil and terrorism. It stands, and its activities fall, very well within the FBI's definition of a terrorist organization.

Background. Boko Haram is a moniker that roughly translates into ''Western education is forbidden.'' But what they really want to do is to establish an Islamic state in Nigeria that is governed under strict Sharia law. Boko Haram adheres to the understanding that Muslims taking part in any secular educational, political, or social activity should be forbidden. In this, they really harken back to the Caliphate of Sokoto and the Empire of before.

Boko Haram came into being in 2002 under the leadership of the charismatic Mohammed Yusuf. Years of recruited followers established a compound in Maiduguri, capital of Borno State. They lived under the Koranic phrase, ''Anyone who is not governed by what Allah has revealed is among the transgressors.''

Yusuf had access to the ruling elite because he came from that class, too. And was indeed financed by them. Subsequent investigations revealed that in addition to Governor Sheriff of Borno, the prominent national politician, Ali Ndume of Borno, too, who was also financial linchpin for the group. There was also a former Nigerian Ambassador, the late Said Upindo who actually was the treasurer, if you want.

Why were these and other prominent Borno politicians involved with this group? Because they wanted to subvert this group and make them part of their election-winning machine. Boko Haram supplied the tax and could coerce voters by force to vote as was desired by this group. So Boko Haram subsequently helped Sheriff win the governorship of Borno State. According to Boko Haram, a tacit understanding was reached with Governor-Elect Ali Modu Sheriff that called for the implementation of a stricter form of Sharia law and the transformation of Borno into a model Islamic state.

A leader of Boko Haram, Alhaji Buji Foi, was appointed to the cabinet of Governor Sheriff. After a year of no movement toward the realization of the promised Islamic state, Mohammed Yusuf asked to withdraw from the governing administration. Alhaji Buji Foi resigned and was eventually killed in suspicious circumstances that Boko Haram said believed was officially instigated. Nineteen members of Boko Haram or sympathizers were mowed down during the burial procession for Alhaji Buji Foi. Therefore, the relationship between the Governor and Boko Haram soured. The Governor then tried to suppress the sect. Open season was declared on the sect.

Inadequately trained police forces responded to threats of challenge to authority by rounding up anyone who they thought might possibly be connected to the annoying group. Usually, that meant sweeping up innocent bystanders in the search for a few guilty men and jailing or disappearing them. When Boko Haram first struck in 2009, the police and others from the administration reacted by raiding their compound and extra judiciously executing the group's leaders including Mohammed Yusuf. In reaction, Boko Haram began a transformation into the terrorist organization that we know today.

In Maiduguri, their home turf, drive-by motorbike assassinations of politicians and policemen became their modus operandi. Their terrorist activities soon ensnarled the rest of the city and in quick order the local security forces could no longer contain them. Boko Haram stepped up wanton killings, bank robberies in and around Maiduguri. When the Federal Government in a ham-fisted manner tried to contain the conflict, the sect turned its eye toward the military and government installations. There have been atrocities and lots of human rights abuses on both sides. But for some notable and very disturbing activities in Kano, Jos, and Abuja, Boko Haram has likely confined their activities to northeastern Nigeria. There is a growing fear that many extremist elements within the sect may try to escalate this crisis throughout the country.

When we talk about Boko Haram, we normally bring up again the Islamist bent and this fear of Sharia. Apart from its engagement in terrorist activities, most disquiet around Boko Haram centers on their expressed desire to create an Islamic state that will be based on strict execution of Sharia laws. With the agitation for Sharia law, Boko Haram managed to focus the public eye on the role of Islam in Nigeria. This spotlight on Islam was enhanced, especially in America after the "Underwear Bomber," Umar Farouk Abdulmutallab, tried to blow up an aircraft that was landing in Detroit on Christmas Day a few years ago. Umar Farouk, of course, is a Muslim from northern Nigeria and would necessarily share cultural and religious traits with members of Boko Haram. Al-Qaeda in Yemen quickly claimed Abdulmutallab and with that sent intelligence analysts scrambling to connect existing and potential dots that may lead to Nigerian groups like Boko Haram.

Most states in northern Nigeria share the same socio-economic, religious and political conditions that would beget a sect like Boko Haram. Indeed, northern Nigeria does have a history of home-grown Muslim sects that present security and administrative challenges to the nation as a whole. We talk about Boko Haram, but before Boko Haram in the 1980s, later 1980s, there were the Maitatsine uprisings centered in Kano, but also radiated from other areas in the north.

In the past decade, two other sects have come into being. This of course is Ansaru, a more radical offshoot of Boko Haram, and of course there is the one that is not talked much about, the Darul Islam sect. But all of them having come on the fact that they adhere to doctrines that move them out of step with the belief structure of the majority of Muslims in Nigeria. But to varying degrees, they do believe that the pervasive corruption in Nigeria and inequality mitigates any real practice of Islam. So for them, established Muslims, especially Muslim leaders cannot be seen as true Muslims, too. This would account for why they killed two Muslims, because they don't see them as true Muslims.

But throughout the history of Nigeria, the rise of sects like Boko Haram has coincided with periods of stark economic stagnation where unemployment is very rife, and inequality grows ever larger. Jobless and angry young men become excellent candidates for fringe groups that teach the necessity to take up arms to create a society based on true tenets of Islam. The glaring injustice, abject poverty, and pervasive hopelessness are the driving forces that create organizations like Boko Haram and MEND in the Niger Delta. Unfortunately, Nigeria with its impressive educated, intellectual class and vast wealth to boot, has so far failed miserably at basically delivering any veneer of good government, justice, economic, and physical security for all of its people.

Economic reports due out next month will show that Nigeria now has the largest economy in Africa, but with a GDP that currently ranks as the 32nd largest in the world, Nigeria is the 156th out of 187 countries on the United Nations Human Development Index. So that is one of the disparities.

Boko Haram attracts discomfort with its talk of Sharia laws. These are edicts that govern morality and lifestyles for the practicing Muslims. Christians, as well as people of other faiths or non-believers have not usually been subject to Sharia law. Admittedly, there have been instances where the insistence of its use create tension between people of different religious backgrounds. Most of the region that is covered by today, northern Nigeria, has been under the sway of Islam for centuries and as such was already subject to Islamic code prior to the colonialization by the British in the early 1900s. Under the British, Sharia law was the law of the land, since of course, the severe and shocking penalties. These trends continued after independence, but developments in the latter part of the last century led to a renewed clamor for the adoption of more stringent Sharia laws. By this time, the monolithic northern region had been carved into numerous states. In the year 2000, several predominantly Muslim slave states in the law and adopted an advanced set of Sharia law as part of the legal systems, despite the concern of the largely Christian population.

So far, the introduction of Sharia law in northern Nigeria have not produced the hoped-for benefits that they wished because, again, the place remains poor. And Sharia law, the way it is applied in Nigeria, it is actually adapted to the cultural sensitivity of the people there, so it cannot produce that.

But in conclusion, when we discuss—here, we talk about the issue of Boko Haram. This question has been discussed in Nigeria too, because at the moment, the question is being asked, ''What is Boko Haram?'' Just like Zenn said, it has morphed into a lot of organizations, a lot of entities with the goal now, the way it is seen in Nigeria, it has been looked upon by certain analysts in Nigeria as being able or capable of making or breaking the nation. Because people in the north, at the moment, we have elections planned for 2015, and seen through that prism, the northerners see Boko Haram as something that was actually created by southerners to create disunity among them.

The southerners look at Boko Haram again from that prism the evil person would say okay, Boko Haram, they are trying to kill us again the way they did during the Biafra crisis. The south—I know I am going overtime. Thank you. But I will answer questions.

[Mr. Nzeribe did not submit a written statement.]

Mr. SMITH. Mr. Nzeribe, thank you very much for your testimony. Just to ask a few questions, let me begin first though with Mr. Adamu.

What was the status and the state of Muslim-Christian relations before Boko Haram? I travel extensively through Africa, but also through other places where there are large Christian and Muslim populations, and in even Sarajevo, before the Yugoslav war, Muslims and Christians had a very close friendship which was then exacerbated by, in that case, the Bosnian Serbs. What was the state of the relation between the two?

Mr. ADAMU. Before the coming of Boko Haram, the Muslims and Christians were united. We are living at peace with each other. During some celebrations, we are sharing food and other things with each other. We live in peace, but the coming of Boko Haram that is where the crisis has started. But before we were living in peace.

Mr. SMITH. One of my biggest takeaways from this trip which reinforced what I thought was the case on the ground was just that, that there was a harmony. There is always some friction, but there were genuine friendships among families and one of the biggest takeaways was how the Muslims are being targeted, not to the extent Christians are. One of our witnesses that was supposed to testify via Skype from the U.S. Embassy in Abuja, but there was some glitch that occurred as of yesterday, not that he didn't want to testify, it was a technical glitch, but Dr. Khalid Aliyu was going to testify here to give a Muslim's point of view on all things as it relates to Boko Haram. That was one of the points that I think is under appreciated in the United States and in the West in general.

These are terrorists who as you just said, Doctor, they do target Muslims, but they have a hatred of all things Christian and it is such a perversion of Islam. One of my close friends in the Islamic community is Reis Ceric, the Grand Mufti of Bosnia. And I will never forget hearing him give a sermon for the reinternment of several, in this case 800, people who died in Srebrenica. And it was a terrible genocide, 8,000 plus people killed in the matter of days, almost all men, separated. It was one of the worst episodes of U.N. peacekeepers ever because they actually helped facilitate it and took no action to stop it as well. So the common cause of Muslims and Christians needs to be emphasized as never before, especially pious Muslims who want no part of what Boko Haram is doing.

One of the questions I asked the Ambassador earlier, Mr. Ogebe, was regarding the victims. What I learned on the trip was that victims of the terrorism are not receiving the kind of assistance from the international community including the United States. Individual, private, voluntary, charitable groups are stepping up to the plate like Voice of the Martyrs and others, but nowhere near approximating the need of these individuals who are now IDPs, have PTSD problems, especially—we met with a child and you will remember this, Mr. Ogebe, who lost his entire family, all slaughtered. He was having a sleepover with a friend when the Boko Haram came to his house and slaughtered his mom and dad, his brothers and sisters and extended family. I mean that little boy, I can't imagine the trauma that he feels, so if you could speak to the victims' assistance that seems to be slim and none.

Mr. OGEBE. Yes, thank you very much, Mr. Chairman. The real concern for us is not only the failure of the state to provide security, but the failure of the state to provide Social Security for victims after they have been victimized. And yes, I do remember that gentleman.

Now what has happened is we have found that the Federal Government, as recently as last week, announced that they will not provide compensation to victims which we find quite unsettling because during your visit, you did mention the victim compensation fund from 9/11, which we thought would be a perfect model for this situation. We have seen this situation get progressively worse where last year we had IDP camps in Jos. Now we have refugees in Cameroon which is a flashback to the Biafra war where so many Nigerians became refugees in Cameroon and never came back, so the impact was felt in neighboring countries around Nigeria. So we do feel that there is a need for the U.S. to help the Nigerian Government to understand that the need to take care of their citizens before and after terrorist attacks.

In conclusion, let me say this. We have an observed situation where the Federal Government of Nigeria has committed to spend about $30 million to repair the U.N. building that was bombed by Boko Haram. And at the same time, turning around and saying well, we are not going to provide compensation to our own citizens who were impacted by this terrible situation.

One last note, the young lady, Deborah, whom you met, the orphan girl whose father and brother were killed in her presence, it was a 9/11 charity in New York that offered for her to come here to trauma treatment after she spent a night tied to the body of her father and her brother. It was average Americans who just cared, who sent for her. And the U.S. Embassy denied her a visa twice. So for us charities who are working on these issues, we are dealing with an unresponsive Nigerian Government in some instances. We are dealing with an unresponsive consulate and we are dealing with terrorists. So it can be very overwhelming.

Mr. SMITH. Thank you. Mr. Zenn, in your ten measures of recommendations, your third one is something I raised with Ambassador Thomas-Greenfield and that was the issue of the Leahy amendment. And I will just quote you in part because I don't think you mentioned this in your oral presentation, but you mentioned,

"Mentor Nigerian troops in counterinsurgency based on best practices learned from years of dealing with IEDs, urban warfare, and ambushes in Iraq and Afghanistan. Currently, the Leahy Act effectively bans U.S. support to Nigeria's Joint Task Force that is fighting Boko Haram. Even JTF units with positive human rights records are blacklisted because of Leahy's wide-reaching ban on entire units—rather than specific abusers. Leahy should be reexamined, or else Nigeria will continue to look to countries like Pakistan for mentorship, which is no recipe for success."

I raised that when I was in Abuja with our leadership there. We had a very good discussion about that. Again, as I mentioned to Ambassador Thomas-Greenfield, I understand the abundance of caution argument, but when it is counterproductive and we can both train true human rights soldiers who have a respect for human rights and also to be more effective at doing their job, it seems to be counterproductive. Could you speak to that?

Mr. ZENN. Right. I wanted to mention this when I spoke about the July 2009 fighting for 4 days between the security forces and Boko Haram which actually led Boko Haram to become the nasty jihadist group that it is today. And it is very true that there were a lot of excesses on the parts of the security forces and it is certain that there are some units of the JTF that have performed human rights abuses. That being said and this comes from people who I know in the security forces as well as people who have witnessed them, there are units that do follow human rights that are committed to human rights and combatting Boko Haram. But it seems that the wide-reaching scope of this is limiting our ability to fight Boko Haram beyond FTO measures which really are on a most broad scale and not the local level. And I understand the logic behind Leahy, but I think we can be more specific and work with those groups that are committed to human rights. And there is no country in the world right now better than the United States who has experienced insurgency for 12 years to mentor them.

And I would also mention that Boko Haram is learning for al-Qaeda around the world, but the Nigerian security forces are not being taught by those are fighting al-Qaeda around the world.

Mr. SMITH. We already have a rather close relationship with their Navy in the south. So there is already a relationship.

Mr. ZENN. There is precedent.

Mr. SMITH. The chilling effect that Leahy inadvertently is having I would respectfully submit is counterproductive. We need to really delve into this and I thank you for your point and as Mr. Ogebe mentioned, Emmanuel mentioned before, he was tortured by the Nigerian military and yet he, too, sees the need for, with proper vetting, doing the kind of training that will truly make the difference. We have learned so much as a country ourselves that ought to be shared, I would think with the Nigerian military.

Mr. NZERIBE. If I may speak to that. At the moment, currently, the Nigerian Government, the Nigerian military is engaged in training units for counterinsurgency operations. Those are units different from the ones now that operate out there. These units, I think they number 3,000 at the moment, the goal is to get them to the forefront to fight. Because even the government recognizes that to fight Boko Haram and some sects you need to give the troops the tools they need to fight.

There was debate going on if they really needed counterinsurgency training or counterterrorism training, but all in all I think they are working toward that angle, that area. I couldn't tell you off my head who is involved in helping with the training. I suspect some Israeli—but they are doing something for that now.

If I may speak to the victim compensation fund, too. It is a topic that is actively debated this time in Nigeria. It has been complicated. As a matter of fact, either yesterday or 2 days ago, the President—well, he finally refused that he was not going to go along with that, but he was just searching for solutions. It has been complicated by the fact that any attempt to create—this is a sticking point—create a victim's fund would attract on the other side to the demand to be involved with it. Boko Haram is still demanding from the Federal Government compensation for killing Mohammed Yusuf today. As a matter of fact, a little while ago there was agreement, they were in discussions first with the Borno State government for cease fire to cease operations and although they asked for 26 billion naira, the Federal Government, Borno State was eligible for foreign aid, but the government said no. It all boiled down to the fact that if they did, they would have to compensate for Mohammed Yusuf.

What has this initiated in the discussion in Nigeria at the moment, they are talking about, okay, you have a group of northern politicians who have taken this now as their own cause. They are saying you refuse to compensate our people, okay, we want Boko Haram to stop fighting. You need to pay them. We are not talking now about the victims, just pay them off, the same way you paid off the many people in the Niger Delta. So they see that as discrimination. And it becomes a rallying point for southern politicians.

Any way you take it, it is really complex, Nigeria, and that is the image that comes through.

Mr. OGEBE. Yes, Mr. Chairman, if I may say something really quickly about this issue of compensation and especially the U.S. argument that this is economic and we need to throw more money at the problem. The ultimate issue here is that the U.S. is opening a slippery slope to the institutionalization of mass murder as a legitimate pathway to more Federal resources. We cannot create a precedent that if you go out and bomb churches, we are going to create a special ministry for you. If the Government of Nigeria could actually consider offering amnesty and finance to Boko Haram to lay down arms, why can't they consider providing compensation for victims? So this is the wrong message that we are sending.

Let me speak again to the military response. I want to emphasize the point that the Nigeria military has served as boots on the ground for the U.S. in situations that the U.S. did not want to go in. In Liberia, where Africa-Americans went back and established that country, the U.S. has strong ties with our country, but it was Nigerian troops and billions of Nigerian money that preserved it. In Somalia, Nigerian troops are there up to this date. Nigeria is contributing to nine U.N. peacekeeping missions. The U.S. is not involved in any of those. So this is a regional power broker that we need. And so the idea that we cannot provide technical assistance to them to deal with the insurgency that they are not used to, but we as Americans have expertise on, is chilling.

In conclusion, let me say that more Nigerian soldiers have died at home at the hands of Boko Haram than have died in the peacekeeping operations in the last 3 years in nine different countries. And so even the U.S. Army had to face a homegrown insurgency here, they would have the same challenges that the Nigerian army is having. We saw what happened with the shooting in Texas when someone turned on Americans who were in their homeland and killed 14 in 1 day.

Let me wrap up my thoughts here by mentioning some of the videos that we couldn't even submit to your committee are chilling. I recently saw a video of Boko Haram decapitating a woman. Generally, it is the people like Adamu Habila fits the prototype. You need to be male and non-Muslim and you will be killed. They usually don't kill the woman. But to see a grown woman who was accused of being a security agent, being decapitated on video and people chanting ''Allah Akbar'' was one of the most disturbing things I have seen. And this kind of explains why the military response is so high handed because what these people are doing is medieval, it comes out of the Stone Age and I do not believe there is any basis for also negotiating with such evil people and offering them money to do this. I think that undermines the rule of law and will end any efforts to maintain a civilization.

Ms. BASS. Thank you very much, Mr. Chairman, and to the whole panel. I just wanted to thank you for your patience. I am sorry. It is always tough and we always complain about it when we have the interruption with votes.

I wanted to ask Mr. Adamu, one, I really appreciate your personal testimony about what happened and the fact that you took the time to come here and share your story. And I just wanted to know if you could talk a little bit more about your area and why it was targeted? Was the whole area a Christian area and it was all being targeted? And then since then, you survived which is amazing, and I am wondering if you—what has happened to your area since then and your family and all that?

Mr. ADAMU. Thank you so much. The Yobe State is one of the major states where the Boko Haram is based. Since the 2011 elections, the Yobe State, we Christians in Yobe State started facing one tenth of the order. Before the attack, before 2011, the Christians that are living in Yobe, we are living like second-class citizens in the state because even though we read, no government can offer appointment for you in order to work. If providential you have appointment to work in the government, you will sit there. The government will not promote you. I am working with the government radio stations. I spent 8 years without promotions, 8 years without promotions. Also, that is what we are facing in Yobe. And also, we are denied to have a land where we build our churches. We are denied to have teachers that can teach our children in school in Christian knowledge. Churches sacrifice in order to pay teachers in order to teach Christian knowledge in Yobe. But they have denied us of all this.

We are also suffering always in our places of work. For example, in the northern part of Nigeria, you have Ministry of Religion Affairs where 100 percent of the staff there are Muslims. Not one Christian is there. You see, this is what continues to happen. When all these things happen, now few Christians that are men arrive. They have fled to the nearest countries, in order to have where they will stay and also the state government started rights to us where we would go back to the state or they would terminate our appointments. Many of the Christians have been terminated their appointments. They are not working now. You see how these people will survive, they are living without work. Now that is why we are calling for a Federal Government to help the northern Christians in order to afford them an appointment to work in the Federal Government. And those that have lost their job, let Federal Government or the state government to give them back their appointment and pay them their money and their salaries.

Ms. BASS. Thank you.

Mr. ADAMU. Thank you so much.

Ms. BASS. Mr. Zenn, you mentioned that Boko Haram, the primary funding is local. And I was wondering what you meant by that? Maybe you can elaborate on that some more, local, how much, from where? And I am asking that in the context of wondering if there is anything that the U.S. can do to be helpful? If it is all local funding, how do we——

Mr. ZENN. Well, I think one thing that is important to consider is that before July 2009, Boko Haram was essentially one of the many, if not hundreds or thousands of Islamists,

Salafist groups in Nigeria and it was fairly mainstream. There was nothing particularly illegal about funding it. The funding streams came through the regular Islamist funding streams, through Sudan, Saudi Arabia, Somalia, and possibly even from Western countries.

So during its rise from 2002 to 2009 when it was propagating its police system which was slightly, but not completely more radical than other groups, it was well-funded. And it even had funding from local politicians that wanted to be on its side because it was a fairly popular group because it had a charismatic leader. And there is already a radical base in northern Nigeria as we have learned.

After 2009, it shifted from being a preaching group to being a bonafide jihadist group with full-fledged violence. And it has become much less tenable for even radical Muslims to support a group like this financially. So I don't think it's going through mainstream funding networks now as much as before, but it has responded by robbing banks. So can we help Nigeria with better bank security? It has kidnapped local people and taken them to safe havens in northeastern Nigeria. Can we help Nigeria to reduce these safe havens, either by providing them with intelligence from the air or better border security? And it has responded by stealing cattle from local people. So again, this goes back to the Leahy argument, what can we do to help Nigeria become more capable and competent of providing security for its own citizens and that will, in turn, reduce its ability to kidnap, exhort, tax local people and fund itself.

And again, our broader al-Qaeda counter funding initiatives might help as well because I do believe this group is connected to al-Qaeda in the Islamic Maghreb and such networks.

Ms. BASS. Thank you. Thank you. And then finally, I wanted to ask Mr. Ogebe and Mr. Nzeribe, it seemed as though when I was listening, Mr. Ogebe when you were talking, unfortunately, I walked in a little bit late, so I wanted to ask a question for both of you to give your perspectives on what the root causes of Boko Haram are, because it seemed as though I heard two different perspectives, but I walked in in the middle of Mr. Ogebe. Because I believe you were disputing the notion that poverty was—you believed was the root cause. So maybe you could both address that.

Mr. OGEBE. Yes. Thank you very much, Ranking Member Bass. I think that there is a reductionist analysis that has oversimplified the deadly theological insurgency and turned it into an ideological, or regional, class warfare. I want to say that there is a lot of poverty in the north. I am from the north, though the middle belt. And there is deep poverty there as well. As a child growing up, my mom asked me to go out and buy half a loaf of bread because we had guests coming. I didn't know it was possible to do that. I walked into the store. They cut it in half and sold me half a loaf of bread. We came from a well-to-do family. My dad was a judge. My mom was a doctor. So there is poverty in the north of Nigeria.

Now the problem here is this. Poor people are some of the most generous people you will ever meet and Muslims are some of the kindest people you will ever meet. So these people who are decapitating women do not remind me of the poor Muslim neighbors I had. I traveled to England once. I came back. My poor Muslim neighbor, I was gone longer than I expected, had gone into my apartment and washed all my clothes before I came back. These are not the people who are out and bombing churches.

Now having said that, I believe that this is an export of an extreme ideology. I will give you a quick illustration. Polio has almost been stamped out as a disease in the world. It is now subsisting in only three countries, Pakistan, Afghanistan, and northern Nigeria. What is the link? We need to ask ourselves these questions.

Ms. BASS. I understand the link between Pakistan and Afghanistan. That is clear. Northern Nigeria?

Mr. OGEBE. If you look at the U.S. terrorism reports, you will find that Pakistan, Afghanistan, and Nigeria rank the same ranking, the top five countries that engage in terrorism. So there is a deep theology where they shoot health workers. The two countries that health workers were shot were Pakistan and Nigeria.

Ms. BASS. Yes.

Mr. OGEBE. So no matter what investments you make, if you don't change his warped mindset and this warped theology, we will have these problems. I will say remember the two Americans who were freed that were kidnapped in the south.

Ms. BASS. Yesterday, right, day before?

Mr. OGEBE. They paid the ransom and they were freed. That is economic. Now in the north, Ansaru kidnapped seven Westerners and executed them, they didn't even bother waiting for ransom.

Ms. BASS. And I do understand what you mean by the export of an ideology, but what is the basis of that ideology taking root?

Mr. OGEBE. The problem is with the interpretation of jihad. Some would believe that it is not a movement, it is not national, it is physical violent jihad. There is another school of thought that says well, when they said kill the Jews and the Christians, it was specific to that time and not to this time. So you need to read it in context. There are others who feel, no, it is universal. We need to keep doing that now.

Let me add that Iran, and this goes back to a question that was asked earlier, Iran has shipped arms to Nigeria. Hezbollah, they just discovered some of their weapons in Nigeria. So all of that activity is going on. The point is this, there are some Shia members that were trained and groomed by Iran who were not satisfied with their nonviolence posture. And so they decamped to form Boko Haram or to join Boko Haram because they felt that this would give them expression to be more violent in their underpinnings. And I believe that Zenn has written a little in this area. So it is not ideology that is really, and the theology that is really, I think, at the core of this problem.

Ms. BASS. Thank you. Mr. Nzeribe.

Mr. NZERIBE. You did hear correctly, there is a difference in the way we look at it. I think it approaches the issue as an advocate and I am looking for broad strokes that actually would help the policymakers come up with policies that can be implemented and on a different level we can talk, other things will come in.

Original Boko Haram, any way you cut and slice it, it is in the conditions, the dire economic conditions in the north. There is huge poverty, but it is almost structural because you have—this goes back actually to the Sokoto Caliphate and when the British came into Nigeria, they discouraged contact and education between Western education. And the British were only happy to indulge them, so they introduced indirect rule. The Emir was responsible. And the Emir goes Western education, we don't need. So that tradition, actually, Boko Haram is in a historical tradition that was always there. But what has happened, especially since the '80s, until the '70s, after the war, the Biafra war, it was masked by the fact, the oil industry boomed and the north actually held sway over the economy of Nigeria. So you had a lot of transfer from the south to the north. And that masked some aspects of a nondeveloping economy that you wouldn't see because it seemed to be money everywhere. But in the '80s, beginning of the '80s, especially since the year 2000, you have had a situation in Nigeria where power shifted in a concrete way from the north to the south. And the establishment, the creation of more states in the north, I think there are 19 states now, they always believed that in the area you hold together, but they began to go their separate way and some would actually make allowances with other states in the south. But effectively, they lost power in the Federal Government.

Why is this important? Because Nigeria is a typical developing country and the government plays a very substantial role in the economy. You don't have the private sector to come to balance and if you control government, you are able to do that. Where I am going is in the north, especially in the '80s, it began to show that they didn't have people who were educated to become part of the economy. They created states that couldn't attract businesses because you didn't have an educated class, so the poverty just kept increasing more and more. They have kids who don't go to school. You have 8-year-olds already in the streets trying to sell things, instead of being in school, so that you get to the point where a kind of helplessness begins to settle in, because in between they see the ruling class is actually doing very well, sending their kids abroad to schools, but refusing to spend money, state money on education for the indigents.

So you get to a point where you have really a lot of poverty, but a lack of skill sets to do anything. And in steps somebody like Mohammed Yusuf who is actually pretty well-educated himself, he is a university graduate, Yusuf steps in and goes up and gathers these people into a compound. He is able to feed them. You feed them. You have the church. You really can work on them. And because they are hopeless anyway, they will do anything for you, anything you tell them. And he says this is it. Just like that was said until the year 2009, Boko Haram it wasn't that terrorist organization because it was more, it was engaged in activities that were on a smaller scale, more akin to what Hamas would be doing in Palestine.

So again, if we look at it on a broader level, it is there, but again, on an individual level, people experience it differently.

Ms. BASS. Thank you very much.

Mr. NZERIBE. You are welcome.

Mr. SMITH. I would like to thank our distinguished panelists for your work and for sharing with us your expertise and insights. It has been most helpful. And I do think your presence certainly helped the administration focus a little harder on designating Boko Haram as a foreign terrorist organization, so thank you for that as well. And is there is anything you would like to say before we conclude, any of our witnesses?

Mr. OGEBE. We want to thank you most kindly, Mr. Chairman, for your leadership on this issue. I honestly believe that if you hadn't taken the issue head on, that we may not have had the conclusion that we had today. So thank you very much for making my Christmas wish come true early.

Mr. SMITH. Thank you. And we will do vigorous oversight and do whatever we can to be helpful and we will revisit and are doing it already with the application or the over application of the Leahy amendment, and I thank you for your insights on that as well and all the others with regards to victims. And this hearing is adjourned and I express my deep gratitude.

Mr. OGEBE. Thank you.

[Whereupon, at 4:01 p.m., the subcommittees were adjourned.]

APPENDIX

MATERIAL SUBMITTED FOR THE RECORD

JOINT SUBCOMMITTEE HEARING NOTICE
COMMITTEE ON FOREIGN AFFAIRS
U.S. HOUSE OF REPRESENTATIVES
WASHINGTON, DC 20515-6128

Subcommittee on Africa, Global Health, Global Human Rights, and International Organizations
Christopher H. Smith (R-NJ), Chairman

Subcommittee on Terrorism, Nonproliferation, and Trade
Ted Poe (R-TX), Chairman

November 12, 2013

TO: **MEMBERS OF THE COMMITTEE ON FOREIGN AFFAIRS**

You are respectfully requested to attend an OPEN hearing of the Committee on Foreign Affairs, to be held jointly by the Subcommittee on Africa, Global Health, Global Human Rights, and International Organizations and the Subcommittee on Terrorism, Nonproliferation, and Trade in Room 2200 of the Rayburn House Office Building (and available live on the Committee website at www.foreignaffairs.house.gov):

DATE: Wednesday, November 13, 2013

TIME: 1:00 p.m.

SUBJECT: The Continuing Threat of Boko Haram

WITNESSES: Panel I
The Honorable Linda Thomas-Greenfield
Assistant Secretary
Bureau of African Affairs
U.S. Department of State

Panel II
Mr. Emmanuel Ogebe
Managing Partner
U.S.-Nigeria Law Group

Mr. Habila Adamu
Survivor of violence by Boko Haram

Mr. Jacob Zenn
Research Analyst
The Jamestown Foundation

Guy Nkem Nzeribe, Ph.D
Partner
Guy Nzeribe Associates

By Direction of the Chairman

COMMITTEE ON FOREIGN AFFAIRS

MINUTES OF SUBCOMMITTEE ON _____ *Africa, Global Health, Global Human Rights, and International Organizations Terrorism, Nonproliferation, and Trade* _____ HEARING

Day __*Wednesday*__ Date __*November 13, 2013*__ Room __*2200 Rayburn HOB*__

Starting Time __*1:00 p.m.*__ Ending Time __*4:01 p.m.*__

Recesses | __*1*__ | (_*1:43*_ to _*2:19*_) (____ to ____) (____ to ____) (____ to ____) (____ to ____) (____ to ____)

Presiding Member(s)

Rep. Chris Smith

Check all of the following that apply:

Open Session ☑   Electronically Recorded (taped) ☑
Executive (closed) Session ☐   Stenographic Record ☑
Televised ☑

TITLE OF HEARING:

The Continuing Threat of Boko Haram

SUBCOMMITTEE MEMBERS PRESENT:

Rep. Weber, Rep. Bass, Rep. Poe, Rep. Sherman, Rep. Brooks, Rep. Perry, Rep. Cotton, Rep. Cook

---

NON-SUBCOMMITTEE MEMBERS PRESENT: *(Mark with an * if they are not members of full committee.)*

HEARING WITNESSES: Same as meeting notice attached? Yes ☑ No ☐
(If "no", please list below and include title, agency, department, or organization.)

STATEMENTS FOR THE RECORD: *(List any statements submitted for the record.)*

TIME SCHEDULED TO RECONVENE _____
or
TIME ADJOURNED __*4:01 p.m.*__

Gregory B. Simpkins
Subcommittee Staff Director